Dancin' with the Devil at Midnight

The true and untold story of the brutal murder of a young black man, Timothy Wayne Coggins, that went unsolved for 34 years and the courage of a family and community that demanded the truth

by Quimby Melton III

3

"Darkness cannot drive out darkness; only light can do that. Hate cannot drive out hate; only love can do that."
Dr. Martin Luther King, Jr.

Dedication

It is to the family of the victim, Timothy Wayne Coggins, as well as the residents of our Griffin-Spalding County community this book is dedicated. This is a community of decent people working together who would not let this evil slaying go unsolved.

For additional information about or copies of this book contact:

Quimby Melton III, POBox 1005, Griffin, GA 30224

qmelton3@gmail.com

or go to:

amazon.com for information on electronic or paperback copies

Amazon ISBN   9781692282264

Profits from the sale of this book will go to:

CASA...a fund that helps Spalding County children with their cases heard within our judicial system

and to .

The Amick Fund...a fund of the Griffin First United Methodist Church that helps citizens of the G/S Community pay their utility bills

Author's Notes

This book is a work of nonfiction. What you will read, as incredible as it is written on these pages, did in fact happen. The events and characters, victims and murderers are all too real.

In certain instances, names have been changed or not given, to protect our sources. For additional security reasons, a few, very few, of the names, locations, items, have been changed, again to protect those involved.

All dialogue within this book is to the best of the recollections of those interviewed. Minor grammatical modifications may have been made to help the reader understand the scene or situation. Transcripts were also used for dialogue within certain chapters. The racial slurs, insults and smears, have been edited or changed out of respect for the family of Timothy Wayne Coggins, the reader, and our community.

This book could not have been written without the help of the ladies in the Spalding County Clerk of Courts office. They, especially Sherry Smith, gave the author invaluable time and help with his record searches and use of the computer.

One of the author's oldest and dearest friends, Don Conkle, works as a title researcher and spends a lot of his time in the Spalding County Clerk's office. I thank him for his assistance in guiding me through the maze of courthouse records.

Also, of note, a special thanks goes to the Spalding County District Attorney's Office. The ladies and gentlemen, the investigators of the DA's office, Ben Coker and Marie Broder, answered numerous questions the author had clearing up information.

The real heroes of this book are the lawmen and women who protect us daily in Griffin and Spalding County. Sheriff Darrell Dix, Captain Mike Morris and the staff steered the author in the direction of the evidence and gave valuable on and off the record quotes and advice.

Judge W. Fletcher Sams runs an orderly courtroom. The author has known Judge Sams and his family most of his life. His mother and father were both doctors in a once rural county. Many times, Doctors' Sams accepted vegetables or eggs in lieu of payment from their patients. They were and are good people. Judge Sams comes from a family that cares deeply about their community. He and his staff, Melanie Nichols, Christy Cornett and Gina Ritchie, the court reporter, kept the courtroom running smoothly.

Bailiffs Barbara Puerifoy, William Matchett and Jim Goolsby did a tremendous job during the course of the Gebhardt trial, even with the overflow crowd of witnesses, interested citizens, family members and media reporters seen entering and exiting the trial daily.

Thanks, respect and commendation goes to Griffin Daily News Reporter Karen Gunnels. Originally from Louisiana, Karen worked there as a journalist. After leaving the teaching profession Gunnels would return to her journalistic roots when she joined the Griffin Daily News staff. The author has great admiration for Gunnels and her accurate writing in this (and other) tough case(s). She is one of the best in her profession.

Many times, if you are lucky, you will meet a person who improves and changes your life. Tom Barrett is such a person to the author. Tom is not only a fine Christian gentleman, but also a bit of a sage. His advice and guidance during the writing of this book was especially valuable and appreciated by the author. Tom, I could not have written it without you!

To my agent, Pamela Harty and The Knight Agency, I could not have found the success without your talents, your guidance but most of all your patience.

The author received wonderful assistance from an established author, Ian Case Punnett. While he was once on late-night national radio followed by millions, he is even better with his written words. Thank you for your direction and helping me find my way within this story.

And lastly, to my family. The author could not have completed this book without them. They were all cheerleaders to the author in this crazy project taken on late in my life. The love of the author's life, my wife Louisa, never let me get confused or off course. My son, Isaac and daughter-in-law Shelly always were interested in the latest twists and turns of the chapters. And my grandsons, Isaac, Jr., Asher and Silas kept my spirits high when they came to play, giving the author's jumbled mind a much-needed break. Thank you, all my darlings.

The author of this book has tremendous respect and appreciation for our legal system and for those who helped bring about justice in this 34-year old cold murder case. The impossible was made possible. My deepest respect also goes to the family of the victim, Timothy Coggins, and of and all our Griffin-Spalding County community. The late crime author Dominick Dunne writes that many times victims get lost in the murder as a trial begins. The focus and attention begin to shift toward the defendant in the courtroom, sometimes even becoming a sympathetic figure. Timothy Wayne Coggins was dead. The shock of this brutal slaying had been absorbed by our community long ago. But Timothy's family…Timothy's courageous family…never forgot this horrendous slaying. They would never let his death be forgotten. Family members were in the courtroom each and every day as a unified force. These are the people who would not let this brutal slaying lie unsolved. It is for our community and the Coggins family this book is written and dedicated.

Lastly, but most important of all, thank you, the reader, for taking your time to read, "Dancin' with the Devil at Midnight." I hope you find it as captivating a story as I did.

OQMIII

Chapters

Dancin' with the Devil at Midnight

The true and untold story of the brutal murder of a young black man, Timothy Wayne Coggins, that went unsolved for 34 years and the courage of a family and community that demanded the truth

Significant Characters *Last name alphabetical order*

Brandy Abercrombie-*Daughter of Bill Moore*

Johnathan Bennett-*Testified at Gebhardt trial*

Marie Broder-*Spalding County Assistant District Attorney*

Sandra Bunn -*Older sister of Frankie Gebhardt*

Lamar Bunn-*Gebhardt's nephew/Sandra's son*

Charles Carey, Jr-*Owner Carey's Mobile Home Park*

Rita Cavanaugh-*Magistrate Judge sent case grand jury*

Harry Charles-*Attorney for Bill Moore*

Timothy Wayne Coggins-*The victim*

Telisa Coggins-*Coggins sister who was at the club*

Heather Coggins-*Niece of Coggins/Family Spokeslady*

Ben Coker-*Spalding County District Attorney*

Jared Coleman-*GBI Special Agent assigned to case*

Linda Morgan Cook-*Coggins aunt-Trio drove up in yard*

Viola Davis-*Timothy Coggins mother*

Darrell Dix-*Spalding County Sheriff*

Robert Lee Dorsey-*Timothy Coggins stepfather*

Patrick John Douglas-*Testified Gebhardt trial*

Carl Elmore-*Griffin Daily News reporter at the scene*

The Coggins Family-*Family of the Victim-In court daily*

Butch Freeman-*Sheriff when Coggins was killed*

Samuel Freeman-*Last person to hear from Coggins*

14

Jesse Gates-*City of Griffin Policeman-Coggins friend*

Franklin George Gebhardt-*Found guilty by a jury*

Jim Goolsby-*Bailiff Spalding County Courthouse*

Karen Gunnels-*Reporter Griffin Daily News*

Ruth Eliz."Mitzie" Guy (Beasley)-*Gebhardt's girlfriend*

Todd Harris-*Spalding County Sheriff's Office*

Ashley Hinkle-*GBI Forensics Biology*

Gregory Huffman-*Jailer arrested for obstruction*

Brent Hutchinson-*Legal defense team*

Atlanta Hydrovac-*Drilled well on Gebhardt property*

Scott Johnston-*Gebhardt Defense Attorney*

Oscar Jordan-*Spalding County Sheriff's Office*

Christina Froehlich Kannon-*GBI Forensics Expert*

Larkin Lee-*Gebhardt Defense Attorney*

William Matchett-*Bailiff Spalding County Courthouse*

Pauline Meyers-*Older sister of Frankie Gebhardt*

William Franklin Moore-*Pled guilty to the murder*

Brenda Moore-*Baby sister of Gebhardt-Moore's wife*

Mike Morris-*Spalding County Sheriff's Office*

Clint Phillips-*Investigator Spalding County Sheriff's Office*

Barbara Puerifoy-*Bailiff Spalding County Courthouse*

Terry Reid-*Inmate duped by Gebhardt*

W. Fletcher Sams-*Spalding County Superior Court Judge*

Willard Sanders-*Gebhardt's friend-found body in woods*

James Sebestyen-*GBI Forensics Biology*

Robert Eugene Smith-*Testified against Gebhardt*

Daniella Stuart-*GBI Special Agent*

Charles Lloyd Sturgill-*Testified against Gebhardt*

Don Taliaferro-*Original Magistrate Judge-Said No Bond*

Warren Tillman-*Medical Examiner*

Chris.Jos.Vaughn-*Testified against Geb.-Found body*

Dr. Virgil Williams-*Spalding County Coroner*

John Wright-*Spalding County Investigator*

Chapter 1
Introduction…Of Another Time

It would take time.

A long time.

Thirty-four years, two hundred fifty-six days and nine hours to be exact.

Hatred, anger, rage, temper, violence, prejudice all take a long time to get over.

To forgive.

To forget.

But most of all it is the resentment, the hurt, the feeling of desperation that has built up inside over the years, the many, many years, that one never gets over.

Tuesday, June 26, 2018, was a day most members of the Coggins family thought would never come. A day they had questioned, time and time again, would they ever see?

A day several family members, including a loving mother and caring stepfather, would never live to see.

But that day finally came, in a small middle Georgia courtroom, in the heat of a glorious summer day.

Their beloved, Timothy Wayne Coggins, nickname "Bug," would find his place in southern history and lore. It would take his life, and sadly death, for a community and family to find peace.

A brutish thug, who had openly bragged about killing that, "n----- boy," a young man he didn't even know, was found guilty. Five counts of guilt. Sentenced to life in prison, plus 30 years. He would never taste sweet freedom again.

The thug's friend, his brother in law, would plead guilty two months later. He would be sentenced to 20 years in prison with another 10- years-probation. The friend would later share that the brute would bring his name up time and again when he was in trouble. Why? Because he chose to marry the murderer's baby sister, rather than party and take part in terrorizing a community. When the brother-in-law pled guilty and was sentenced the judge was not happy even though he followed a request by the family and law enforcement. The judge wanted the killer to spend more time in jail. But it was time for this trial to be over and allow a community to heal. Afterall it has been a long, long 34 years before justice's day was found.

A crime that had rocked the small middle Georgia town, was quickly swept under the rug 34 plus years ago. Even the elite Georgia Bureau of Investigation had lost key evidence, had turned to other matters, and then had simply forgotten about the murder. For after all, it was the murder of, "just another black man."

It took a relentless sheriff, an unyielding district attorney's office and a hamlet of people who became tired of the threats the bully made to bring peace to a grieving family.

Prejudice is defined as a, "prejudgment. Forming an opinion before becoming aware of the relevant facts of a case. The word is often used to refer to preconceived, usually unfavorable, judgments toward people or a person because of gender, political opinion, social class, age, disability, religion, sexuality, race, ethnicity, language, nationality or other personal characteristics."

Racism, however, is different. Racism is, "directed against someone of a different race based on the belief that one's own race is superior."

Thirty-four years, two hundred fifty-six days and nine hours later, prejudice in the small middle Georgia town would change. The murder was of another time, another era, a different type of prejudice.

Evildoers have been with us forever. But why? What makes them act in their wicked ways?

Even after he was found guilty by a dozen members of the community, the hatred, anger, bigotry, the racism would remain inside the murderer. He simply did not understand why it was not accepted or against the law to kill a young black man.

As the sentence was read, the murderer, the racist, the bully, the thug would curse and hiss. His inner hatred and racism will never die.

This is the story of three young men, a victim, a murderer and a friend whose lives intertwine time and again. They barely knew each other. All had been born and grew up in the small southern town. All lived a short eight miles from each other along the once mighty railroad tracks. But their societies and their worlds were thousands of miles apart.

This is their story. The story of how prejudice changed in the small southern town.

This is the story of how good will triumph over evil, each, and every time.

"Do not be overcome by evil, but overcome evil with good" Romans 12:21

Chapter 2
Black eyes without a soul

The accused looked at the reporter sitting close enough see the unshaven hair standing on the neck of the overweight, bald, brutish man.

His eyes. black, hollow, piercing. These were definitely the eyes of someone that had lost his soul. The eyes were hollow, without any sign of compassion or remorse. They lay in the skull without movement, without any point of reference. Without a point of return.

The eyes…they simply stared.

It had been 34 long years since a young black man, "just another black man," had been brutally stabbed, drug behind a truck, and left dead in a rural patch of weeds in the hinterlands. A jury finished listening to days of testimony, gruesome, unnerving, horrendous testimony about the murder. They were set to return to the courtroom and give their guilty or not guilty verdict.

Confident as ever, the accused sat with an air of assurance. Alongside his two defense attorneys who knew the consequences of a guilty verdict and appeared somber. Two of the best defense lawyers money could buy, well not the accused's money but the money of family members. He was sure of his innocence. Many in the courtroom were not.

Who knew which side the jury would accept as the truth?

But those eyes. Those black soulless eyes, they glared and looked out into the void.

The defense lawyers had fought the prosecution point by point and had offered a convincing defense. But would it be enough, enough to convince the jury? Enough to allow the bully to once again taste freedom, and plant fear into those he knew had turned him into the law…this time.

On the left-hand side of the courtroom, facing the judge, next to the jury box, the state and prosecution anxiously awaited word. Assistant District Attorney Marie Broder and her team had gone over every shred of evidence, every piece that had not been lost after a long 34-year lapse between the murder and today. Testimony had been given by both professional criminologists and detectives, as well as mutts of the community, who themselves had been in and out of the penal system of Georgia. It had been like a championship, 15 round prize fight. Defense and prosecution had given it their absolute best.

Everyone in the courtroom, the victim's family members, the spectators, the media, the accused's family, the law enforcement wondered. Wondered what the verdict would be?

Everyone but Franklin George Gebhardt.

What did the accused think as he confidently sat close to the reporter?

He had gotten out before. No doubt he would be out again. It was just the way it was. His oldest sister, Sandra, had protected her younger brother time and again. Felonies, and misdemeanors, a rap sheet of several dozen crimes. She had always gotten him out of trouble. In her eyes he could do no wrong.

But in the eyes of society and justice he revolved in and out of jail for threats, parole violations, and fights with the women he had bedded.

Franklin George Gebhardt was just that way.
A misfit, a thug, a bully who had gotten his way most of his life, through threats, intimidation and physical violence. He simply didn't care. Afterall he had protected the white race. That's what he had been taught as a young boy when he first peeked into the meeting of his like-minded oddballs, the brothers of the Ku Klux Klan.

"This was just another n----- boy," the brute thought to himself. "He ain't worth shit."

There was no way a jury would come back and convict him of something that had happened 34 years ago. No way.

With an air of confidence, the tyrant smiled to himself.

But his eyes. They pierced through the justice within the small Georgia courtroom.

The year 1959 or 1960

Born in Sunnyside, Georgia, a small hamlet within Spalding County, Franklin (Frankie) George Gebhardt screamed his first breaths of life on August 19, 1959 (or 1960) depending on who you are talking to. As the fifth child and third son of Charles and Evelyn Gebhardt, Frankie was down the rung of the ladder as far as care and concern. But Frankie had friends nearby whenever he wanted to play.

This was a southern mill community. In what began in the late nineteenth century, Griffin soon became known as, "Towel Town," supplying towels to the world. Employing thousands of those within the Griffin and Spalding County workforce for over a hundred years. But hard times were coming. Closure of the cotton manufacturers began in the mid 1990's. Cheaper labor could be found overseas.

Charles Gebhardt, the patriarch of the family would find work at Compton Highland Mills. His wife, Evelyn, was a housewife. The mills would support the family of seven, that would soon become eight. Frankie was the baby child, until a sister, Brenda was born. Older siblings included sisters Pauline and Sandra. Older brothers were Richard and Charles.

Play for Frankie was often with old worn out toys, things with wheels, many times missing a wheel or two. Little Frankie, however, enjoyed the outdoors. He liked being in or near the woods. He found the birds, the squirrels, the small animals exciting and fun to be around. Frankie was loved and well cared for, mainly by his older sisters Pauline and Sandra but he also learned early that he would have to take care of himself, either by his fists or his mouth. These were fun and happy times. But as the years would roll along and he got older, Franklin George Gebhardt would never really be happy again.

Frankie was small for his age, eventually reaching a height of only five feet, six inches tall. Because of his small statue he quickly found out how to take care of himself, Frankie was a bully most of his life. It was his lot in life. Gebhardt's Zodiac sign is Leo. If you believe in this kind of destiny according to the stars, horoscopes describe Leos as people "who can be very proud and self-centered. They can be bossy. They are not afraid. Leo's are known to speak their mind. You may be misunderstood and have a gift for reading people. Be careful...you have the likelihood to exaggerate sometimes."

Even though Frankie had a brood of siblings to depend on, and friends within the Sunnyside village, he suffered in school and found it boring. The structure and rules didn't fit into Gebhardt's grand plan of life. Attending the Sunnyside Elementary School, which no longer stands, Frankie dropped out of the formal education system in sixth grade. Even though school attendance is compulsory in Georgia until age sixteen, education officials did not seek out the young boy after he quit. A twelve-year old boy on his own, Gebhardt would find many things to peak his interests.

Throughout his life, Frankie Gebhardt claimed could not read nor write. This was not creative ambivalence, it was true. As an adult he had to depend on family and friends to sort his mail, throwing out the junk reading to him what was important. It is not known if Gebhardt had some sort of dyslexia and was not able to function within the traditional educational system. In today's modern school, instructors and clinicians would have been able to evaluate the boy quickly. He may have been placed in what is called special needs classes. But this was 1971-72, and the school system then was not equipped for the type of screening needs readily available today. We just don't and may never know exactly why Frankie dropped out at such an early age. But the fact of the matter is, he dropped out.

Who knows when the festering anger, the meanness, the hatred of others began in the mind of the young boy? But when it began it would explode and remain in his bones for a lifetime.

William (Bill) Franklin Moore, Sr. became Frankie's brother-in-law when he married Frankie's baby sister, Brenda. Years later Moore would recall in an interview, "Frankie was always mean. He was always a bully. I don't know why? He was just always mean."

Moore continued, "Frankie always had to build himself up and try and put my name into stuff and get me in trouble. He (Frankie) was a bad ass for sure."

Perhaps Frankie resented the fact Bill began coming around his home to visit his baby sister. Bill had wheels. Frankie did not.

"Frankie wanted to party and wanted to hang around and stuff," Moore told the author. "But I wanted to see his sister (Brenda). I didn't (want to) marry that boy (Frankie)!"

Apparently, Frankie begrudged the fact so much that one time he picked up an axe when Bill was at his house with his back turned. "He was coming at me with the axe," Moore said. "He probably would've killed me if his mama (Evelyn) hadn't called out and told him to put the axe down." Another time Frankie got so mad at Bill when he was courting Brenda, he picked up a brick and threw it at his windshield and broke it. "My mother (Barbara Jean) made him pay for that windshield," Moore remembered.

Gruff, rough, corn cob of a man

There is no tender way to explain the personality of Franklin George Gebhardt.

"Frankie," the name used by family and friends, is a gruff, rough, corn cob of a man. Gebhardt liked to drink and lived to enjoy sexual partners. Gebhardt would also become a murderer.

Beer or whiskey, it didn't matter. It was all to get drunk. The cheaper the brand the better because Frankie could drink even more. His preference, Jack Daniels Whiskey.

This was the brand of the outlaws, the bandits, the "real men." When Frankie took his first drink, well under the legal age of twenty-one, Frankie knew he had found his elixir.

Frankie came on to women and women came on to him. The women Frankie would enjoy the pleasures of the flesh with were all white. He, nor what would be his, "old lady," at whatever time, wanted anything to do with blacks. "N------ ain't worth shit," Frankie could be heard to say time and again. Most of the women and men that hung around with Frankie liked to drink and fornicate as well. Both Frankie and his old ladies were convenient partners to each other, long enough to get some primal needs out of their system.

If he and his friends, men or women, could afford it, cocaine, marijuana, mushroom tea and even a tablet or two of speed, were quickly consumed. These were the drugs of choice in the 1980's. But these were expensive for the close-knit band of marauders. Sometimes the drugs were taken on their own. Most of the time the drugs were taken with a gulp of beer or whiskey. It gave a better high and rush for the night ahead. All the spirits and drugs were taken early and often as the evening progressed and whatever inhibitions there may have been were abandoned.

Frankie Gebhardt worked hard all his life. But it was not for fulfillment, for fame or fortune. Frankie worked because the money he made gave him a chance to drink and copulate and drink. Rough and wild could be adjectives used to describe the type of life Gebhardt lived. Hard-hard living and even harder drinking were parallels that consumed most of Frankie's waking hours. A stupor would begin in the wee hours of the morning lasting well into the day. A drunken stupor was the only rest Gebhardt would find.

But like many who drink for a living, Gebhardt could bounce back quickly. It took a toll on not only Frankie physically, but also mentally. But the real downward spiral Franklin George Gebhardt found himself in was internally ingrained. He hated African Americans, then called blacks, with a passion. Gebhardt saw the progress blacks were making in his corner of paradise and he did not like it.

He didn't like it whatsoever.

Blacks who had worked the most menial jobs for eons in the south began to be afforded the privileges once only meant for white people. When Frankie was growing up into a young man of legal age, the rules and boundaries all changed. Blacks began eating in restaurants, drinking out of the same water fountains, sitting in the same waiting rooms and even occasionally dating a white woman. This could be done in Atlanta, which was 40 miles to the north of Griffin. But inner-racial dating or marriage was not approved in Frankie's home community.

This was the last straw for Gebhardt.

As he saw these changes his rage and anger grew. "It ain't right. These damned n------ f---ing our women," Gebhardt related to his friends many times. Perhaps this, or an even deeper spirit or belief, shoved Frankie headlong toward Ku Klux Klan membership. These were simply the "type," of people Franklin George Gebhardt understood. An understanding that came early in his life.

+++++++

As he sat confidently awaiting the jury's return, Gebhardt looked toward the reporter who was directly in front of him, perhaps six to seven feet away.

The reporter caught another quick glimpse into the cold black eyes of the accused killer.

Those eyes. Those cold, dark, soulless evil eyes.

There was no happiness. No joy. No mercy. No understanding in these eyes.

There was no soul inside the body of the man named Franklin George Gebhardt.

He had danced with the Devil a long, long time ago.

Chapter 3
Different lives…Eight miles apart

How does a killer justify murder?

They can't.

A stranger you don't even know, mutilated like an animal in the middle of the night.

You don't even know the victim, well not really.

But you heard the stories. Are they true? They must be true.

Doesn't matter. You heard the stories.

A black man danced with a white girl.

You heard talk that same black man had sex with a young 14-year old white girl maybe even your baby sister.

A drug deal had gone bad.

Can't be. Mustn't be.

Your anger, your rage, your viciousness takes over any judgement you may have had. It's your sacred duty to stand up. You are part of the superior race. You are white. You are going to, "kill that n-----."

Even though you can't read or write, you are smart...street smarts. You were raised that way.

You are smart enough to hide evidence, to baffle law enforcement, to get away with the murder...for 34 long years.

That is until one day...that one fateful day when it all came crashing down.

Impossible!

Unbelievable!

This story is true.

Griffin is a small town located in the middle of Georgia

Griffin, Spalding County, Georgia, is a peaceful community. Neighbors know each other. People are friendly. Families eat at church picnics together. Sons and daughters play sports together, are in school together, and laugh when they tell each other jokes at the "Korn Dawg," booth at the yearly October fair. Law enforcement keeps order. Arrests are made soon after a crime is committed. The judicial system punishes the guilty quickly and severely. African American, white, Hispanic work toward a better place to live, work and play.

But in 1983, things were different. A hideous murder was committed. An anger filled white man killed, "just another black man." It was a turbulent time in the south. But thanks to the leadership, both black and white, Griffin and Spalding County was more racially tolerant, and matters were more diffused than in many other Georgia communities. However, the fact is, an unspeakable murder had occurred. What the law enforcement and community quickly forgot; a family always remembered…remembered for a long 34 years.

Prejudices eventually change.
Even in the south.

But racial hatred…it never dies. North, south, east or west, the anger, the fear, the abhorrence is as alive as ever. We simply have not learned to trust or listen to each other.

Timothy Wayne Coggins grows up in Griffin

Timothy Wayne Coggins was born into a simple, hardworking household on, Monday, August 29, 1960. His mother, Viola Dorsey, was a kind and patient housewife. His father was Marshall Lawrence. Robert Lee Dorsey is listed as Timothy's stepfather at the time of his death. Robert Lee was a bus driver for the school system and from all indication a very good one at that.

He took good care of his stepchildren and young passengers.

Timothy also grew up in a large family of eight children. Coggins had four sisters: Peggy (Richard), Harriette Coggins, Telisa Coggins and Jackqueline (Blash). His three brothers were: Tyrone Coggins, Raymon Coggins and Eugene Coggins who would later be killed at the Spalding County jail after an arrest, but that's another story.

The family lived in a simple home along East Solomon Street in Griffin. Downtown Griffin was only a few blocks west making it easy for the young Timothy to walk to where "excitement could be found." Life was not easy for the family, but it also was not as hard as many found in the small southern town. Walking past the A&P Supermarket, American Mills, the Griffin Daily News, Griffin Sales and Service, the old Griffin Police Department, one crisp fall morning, the eight-year old Timothy had to remember what life was like in the 1960's south. Tensions between black and white were high since the assassination of Dr. Martin Luther King, Jr. on April 4, 1968. But as for tensions between the races in Griffin, it was lessened by both the black and white leadership of the town. Still there were mean, taunting white folks in the town and county. These men, and sometimes women, were not to be messed with. The town had separate drinking water fountains, one for white and a dirtier one for "coloreds." Many of the waiting rooms were still segregated. Even the Trailways bus station next to the Griffin Daily News, had a white and, "colored," waiting room for its passengers.

The lunch counters at the McClellan's and Woolworth's in town were getting use to the idea of serving black customers. It was not violent in the town, but then again, what was accepted, and normal today, was not normal or accepted back then. While the young Coggins lad had to watch his steps and be careful, he could have not imagined that this hate and despicable feelings would find him lying in an unmarked grave fifteen years later.

Once Timothy began school, he rode the school bus, maybe even the one his stepfather drove, to Susie B. Atkinson School. Several of the passengers and friends, both black and white, who rode with Coggins on the bus remembered him as a, "real nice guy. He was a lot of fun to be around. Always joking and talking. No, he was not shy at all."

Timothy Wayne Coggins was classified as, "Special Ed," in school. The exceptionality never noted in his records. Special education services in the 1960's and 1970's was not as progressive or encompassing as they are today. So, Timothy too may have struggled in school. We simply do not know. But what we do know is that he was a friendly young man who wanted to please others. Timothy enjoyed people. He enjoyed talking, singing, but most of all dancing. It was all about the dancing. Timothy loved the sounds and moves of the Four Tops, The Temptations, Gladys Knight and the Pips. But perhaps his favorite singer was Philadelphia born Frankie Beverly. Beverly's slides, his mastery of song and dance with his band Maze was something to behold. The vinyl records in Coggins home played these songs over and over and over. Now nicknamed, "Bug," because he danced like a, "little jitterbug," Coggins mastered the smooth moves and steps of his hero, Frankie Beverly. Later, these dance moves would cost "Bug," his life.

Though he had never seen any of these acts up close, he had heard family and relatives talk about, "The Chitlin' Circuit." This was a circuit of black entertainers who performed their music with one-night stands in many of the small towns that dotted the textile communities of the South. Griffin had been on the, "Circuit." Raucous little-known performers such as Rufus Thomas sang about, "Big Fine Hunk of Woman." Barbara Carr, with her sultry howl cried, "Stroke It." Charles Wilson remembered his one time, "Backdoor Lover," in his songs. Even the now well-known, who would later become super star entertainers, earned their performing chops in these forgotten venues. Otis Redding, Little Richard, Ike and Tina Turner would start on the circuit. Night after night, another young man, James Marshall, worked these venues with Slim Harpo, Carla Lewis, Ironing Board Sam, Nappy Brown and Bob Fisher and the Barnesvilles. He would soon become guitar god, Jimi Hendrix. They all performed night after night, for little to no pay. What these performers got stiffed in pay they gained in experience, worth later millions, entertaining mostly black, hometown crowds.

Only eight miles up the tracks from Griffin lies Sunnyside. Things are far different in Sunnyside than where Timothy grew up.

Hate and distrust

Eight miles up the road in Sunnyside blacks were not welcome. The court ordered integration of schools, cafeterias, motels in the name of equality did not sit well with many, particularly Franklin George Gebhardt. He was now finding the lexicon of the KKK to his liking, filling his passion with hate and distrust. It was not about equality to Gebhardt or his friends, it was about the superiority of the white man and white race. These bastions of Southernhood were not to be messed with by any judge or court.

Within the turbulent 1960's and 70's, things in the south began to change. In what had been a predominant "white only," environment, integration, desegregation, equal employment was now afforded to all, black and white. Frankie and his family began to see that black and white were competing for the same jobs at the cotton mills. And for most in the town, this was good, stable money to bring home. Cotton products were flying off the shelves and the center of the trade was Griffin, GA.

The Ku Klux Klan, derived from the Greek word, "kyklos," meaning circle, has been a part of our nation since the Civil War. Formed in 1866 by a group of Confederate veterans as a social club in Pulaski, Tennessee, supporters argue the society protects women and children. All is good…if you are white. The reality with the modern-day Ku Klux Klan is that this is an extremist, violent, sub-culture intent on hatred, maligning and violence toward African Americans or their supporters. Today the Southern Poverty Law Center identifies a total of nine hundred fifty- four hate groups within the United States, seventy-two such groups being associated with the KKK. Four groups of KKK supporters can now be found in Georgia; two statewide (Loyal White Knights of the Ku Klux Klan and the Sacred Knights of the Ku Klux Klan); one in Cedartown (International Keystone Knights of the Ku Klux Klan); and one in Ellijay (United Northern and Southern Knights of the Ku Klux Klan). Back in the day when Frankie was growing up, the Experiment area of Spalding County, located near the major mills of the town, was the center of the secret, but known, Klan meetings.

Usually meeting in a small diner next to the railroad tracks in Experiment, the Spalding County Klan would plot, scheme and plan their menacing activities. Perhaps Frankie snuck into one or two of these meetings finding this vile and abhorrent language to his liking. All too soon Gebhardt would become a dependable member of the local chapter, if not on any "official" roll but with his dedicated and unwavering loyalty. Frankie bragged more than once he, "hated n------." Nothing would have suited Frankie Gebhardt more than to be included, for once in his life, with a group of other hateful ragamuffins. He could have in fact been the poster boy for the KKK; Angry, rough, uneducated, and most of all...white. This "education," from the Klan would be the start of Gebhardt's troubles with the law.

Frankie had met the devil and signed a pact to help Satan's do business here on earth.

An outdoor advertising sign, just north of Sunnyside along the Atlanta Highway 19/41, proclaimed, "Impeach Earl Warren." Warren had been the Chief Justice of the U.S. Supreme Court when the decision that segregation was against the Constitution was made. A fiery, ultra conservative group, the John Birch Society, had paid for the sign. Not as derisive a group as the KKK, it still showed the contempt the "right" people had for their government. Things were not peaceful or idyllic at all as Coggins or Gebhardt approached manhood.

William Franklin Moore, Sr.

One of the friends that Frankie hung around with was Bill Moore. Moore whose full name is William Franklin Moore (later Sr.,) was just as hard a worker, hard a partier and hard a woman chaser as his friend Frankie. One could even say that Bill was Frankie's, "wing man." Often Bill would dive deeply into the trouble that Frankie found, and vice versa. A definite simpatico existed between the two men, all their lives.

It is interesting how the lives of Franklin George Gebhardt and William Franklin Moore (Sr.) intertwined. Both shared the name Franklin in their birth name. Both grew up in lower class environments. Both had drinking problems. Both were in and out of jail, probation and found themselves, or depended on family member, to pay fines for their illicit behavior.

Frankie had both a son and daughter out of wedlock. The son, Franklin Cory Gebhardt, would turn out much like his old man, in and out of jail. The daughter,** (see notes at end of book), married into a prominent family in Griffin and tried to leave her past behind.

Both Frankie and Bill had a wife die. And to put the cherry on top of the sundae, Frankie and Bill were brother in laws.

But it was Frankie, definitely Frankie, the bully Zodiac Leo, who called the shots when Bill was around. Bill seemed to be intimidated and unsettled by his friend. Most of the time Bill did Frankie's bidding. Both for good and bad never questioning the morals or validity of Frankie's orders.

Carey's Mobile Home Park

In the south, as in many regions of the United States, modular housing meets the housing needs of many Americans. There are Mobile Home Parks that have numerous facilities. There are parks that cater mainly to the retired. There are parks that are near the seashores of our nation filled with numerous amenities.

And then there are, "trailer parks." Trailer parks are where the action is…where the music is loud. Where trucks and cars sit idle, unable to crank, in yards filled with junk, old mattresses, worn out plastic kiddie pools, fast food trash and rusty old bar-b-que grills. If money is used to repair a vehicle that is beyond its years in useful driving, it means no groceries will be on the table. If a paycheck is missed disaster declared. Children play in retention ponds nearby. Some even laugh and call them the, "do-do pond." Trailer parks, not the modern landscaped mobile home park, is a place for people to go when they are at the end of their rope, but don't know it.

To call Carey's Mobile Home Park adequate housing, or even a trailer park, would be blasphemy to any ratings system and sacrilege to the mobile home industry. Carey's caters to people that need temporary housing and have permanent problems. Rents are paid by the week, never by the month.

Law enforcement despised being called to the Sunnyside facility to handle domestic disputes, (mostly) drunk and disorderly, serve subpoenas, or break up fights. The wickedness found at Carey's was of the ages. Sodom and Gomorra come in a distant second place when the parties began at Carey's. Yet on Friday and Saturday night, really any night for that matter, Carey's was where drunks and druggies began their party, took a breather and ended just before the sun came up across U.S. Highway 19/41. The rougher the better. The more outrageous the accepted. Drugs, alcohol, sex and hard-core Southern rock and roll knew the worn pathways of Carey's very well.

During the early 1980's, Franklin George Gebhardt lived both in and around Carey's "Mobile Home Park." It was not that Frankie was down on his luck. He always had jingle and folding money in his pocket. He worked hard at the local mill(s), as a repairman, as a pulp-wooder. One prominent Griffin family, who hired Frank Gossett to do repair work at their home, of which Frankie Gebhardt was employed, said, "Frankie did real good carpentry work. Really excellent. He was quite good at what he did."

The problem was Frankie partied even harder. It was as if it was in his blood, his DNA, his expectations and desires. Maybe because he was short, a bully, a Leo's mans-man Frankie had to prove he could out drink, out snort, out fornicate anyone and everyone in his group of friends. "He was an animal when it came to partying. There was no quit in Frankie," remembers one of his hombres who asked his name not be used. During the day you would work. During the night you would party. Life was simple, if you have the "right (and white) stuff."

In the 1980's there was little growth in the Sunnyside area. The main highway from Griffin to Atlanta, US Highway 19/41, ran right through the middle of the hamlet. Downtown Atlanta was a forty-five-minute drive away. There were lots of country backwoods where Carey's ended. Miles and miles of empty land. Georgia Power electric lines crisscrossed the area, because it was rural, but mainly because the landowners were glad to take the plump monthly rental check from the power company to their bank.

This was no man's land. Desolate, isolated, on the main highway but years away from real civilization.

A few landowners did grow crops, soybean and such. Some farmed pine trees. A few more raised cattle. Few to no houses could be found in the area at the time.

The year 1983

In 1983 Timothy Wayne Coggins turned 23 years old. Franklin George Gebhardt was exactly one year and ten days older. Integration continued to rub Gebhardt's skin. Gebhardt would tell an admiring crowd of fellow and would be Ku Klux Klanners at a "get together rally," near Experiment he was, "against n------." Ever since he had quit school, Gebhardt planned and plotted how he would get even with what he called many times the, "inferior" race. He and his friends would do whatever immoral deed they could to scare and intimidate the local black population. Regretfully the black population had little to say when it came to enforcement of the law. Sure, there were good people in Griffin, those who genuinely did believe times had changed for the better. Times where men were truly equal. But, often, the courts and law enforcement looked the other way if a crime had been committed toward a black.

Gebhardt and his KKK thugs flew well under the radar for many years when it came to prosecution.

Frankie was beginning to be well known by the judicial and penal system in the State of Georgia. Earlier, on January 29, 1983, Gebhardt had been arrested by the Henry County Sheriff's Office for "Criminal Damage in the Second Degree." The case would go through the court system, eventually being adjudicated in November,1984. Gebhardt was convicted and would begin a four-month term in prison for the damage. His life would never be the same as a mug shot with numbers underneath was taken when he was arrested (*see photographs of the mug shot at end of book*).

Getting an even earlier start within the penal system was his buddy, Frankie's, "wing man," Bill Moore. Bill liked his liquor. By 1978, Moore was well known to area law enforcement. Moore had been arrested numerous times for "Habitual (DUI) Violator." His Georgia Driver's License was taken from him when he was 17 years old. He would not officially get it back until he was 40. But that did not keep Bill off the road. He would do his obligatory probation, pay fines and serve jail time all before he turned 20 years old.

+++++++

Three young lives living only eight miles apart.

All three just starting out.

Three lives that would take far different paths.

For the youngest life would end before it began.

For the other two, the beginning would be the end, 34 years later.

Chapter 4

A gathering in the graveyard on New Year's Eve

December 31, 2017

Cornered in the southeastern side of the cemetery stands a new headstone. This is the tombstone of Timothy Wayne Coggins. The new year, 2018, is only hours away. In what has been a tumultuous year for the Coggins family the beginning of the end has finally come. It is the last day of 2017. The mighty Georgia pines and oaks stand tall and erect, swaying with each gust of the winter wind. Fallen leaves scatter.

The late December day was crisp, like many early winters in Georgia can be. Not cold but crisp. Through the one hundred thirty-six seasons, winters, springs, summers and falls, acorns have dropped onto the damp ground, growing into trees ever reaching toward the heavens as does the spire of the small community church in front of the graveyard.

Tonight, would be like most of the others. The family had grown. Some members into women with their own children. Some into older adults who remember what it had been like, "back in the day," when respect was taken but never given. Family children heard stories and tales about what happened to the young man, barely twenty-three years old. Their grandparents told them about the hatred, the anger, the murder of one of their own. Too young to really understand, but old enough to know why. They too cried tears, but wondered, always wondered why it had happened? This murder was hard for all to grasp. This was not fiction but truth, fact, reality.

 An early evening twilight began to creep in over the horizon. Today had been a good day...no it has been a great day!

The usual procedure of the family was to visit the grave, remember the dead, say a prayer, then move on from the unmarked grave. Buttons, coins, an occasional bit of bone, mostly from the animals that lived in the nearby woods, could be dug up from the acre around the Fuller Chapel United Methodist Church graveyard, a small African American church in a small southern town.

Today's service would last around ninety minutes. Tyrone Coggins, brother of the slain family member, helped coordinate this special day. Family members wore purple ribbons, Timothy's favorite color. All had chipped in to buy the memorial marker.

Fuller Chapel United Methodist Church has stood as a beacon for the African American community in this small

Georgia town for decades. Just up the road, on one of the main streets, sits the mostly white First United Methodist Church of Zebulon. Fuller Chapel has seen dynamic social and political change since it was established. The members, many who are buried in the church cemetery, are witnesses to this change. They too had felt the indignity, the sorrow, the despair that only the African American community could feel during turbulent times. Headstones, some marked, most not, line the field. They are gravestones and memorials to the fallen church members who have witnessed many of these events themselves.

Tonight, would be the same…but different. This afternoon, the family would once again honor their own. Stories told, tears shed, prayers lifted. But tonight…tonight also offered one thing that had been missing for 34 years…hope.

Hope that the murder of their brother, their nephew, their friend, would be solved in the coming new year. There had been talk 34 years ago of a horrible, angry, bull of a man who went into a rage. Stories how this monster and his friend stabbed the young black man of 23 years and then dragged him behind their truck. A dying young black man drug over the rocks in the field…over and over and over. Drug through the brush to a spot under power lines that ran above what was an off beaten path. There had even been tales of how the man, who could not read or write, had carved an "X" into the back of the victim. These were horrible tales making younger family members cringe, but older members remember.

This had been an unspeakable murder of, "just another black man." His mistake was dancing with a white woman, which is something you did not do if you were a young black man in 1983, living in a small southern textile town.

But tonight, things were the same…but yet, different.

A family loved one, Timothy Wayne Coggins, has finally been laid to rest. Tim made it home.

In 1983 the burial had been a hurried, fearful affair. Family members didn't know if they too would be targeted, simply because they were black. It didn't seem possible that this young man, only 23 years old, was brutally and savagely murdered. Many this day remember their beloved own, Timothy Wayne Coggins, nicknamed, "Bug," because he was, "like a little jitterbug." Timothy was full of life, someone who loved to dance and sing and enjoy life…but also someone who lay in that cold grave under a cold blanket of concrete. Timothy was yet to make his mark in this world. And yet, "just another black man's," life had ended oh, too soon.

Tonight, was the first time Timothy Wayne Coggins lay beneath a fine marble headstone. The whole world now knew his name and who he was and when he died. Before, he, along with the dozens of others in the graveyard, had an unmarked concrete slab as a blanket. The family was fearful, that perhaps if known, the grave would be desecrated by these murderous men and their friends. Men, and some women, filled with hate. It was all about a race they reviled, simply because they were not white like them.

After 34 years, without an answer, the Coggins Murder Case had the promises of being solved. Courageous investigators, a sheriff and his deputies had uncovered evidence that was shunned aside 34 years ago because it was the death of, "just another black man."

Tonight, a family had hope. Hope that murderers would be brought to justice by a relentless district attorney and his staff. Hope that after all these years they would find peace. After all these years the real story would be told with all its unpleasant, gory, horrid details.

Yet hope…hope is written in the future tense.

Within a few hours a new year would begin with all the promise of the future tense.

Some graves are marked but many, about half, remain unmarked. Those buried souls known only to history and to God. But all had a sense of joy on this most special day. One of their own is now known. Timothy Wayne Coggins has been identified and his family is ready to continue their fight for justice in the months that lie ahead.

The new headstone stands proud and tall in the cool night air of New Year's Eve. A headstone all the world will soon know about. "Timothy Wayne Coggins, born August 29, 1960, died, October 9, 1983. Gone, but never forgotten. In loving memory," etched into the once uneven marble.

The Coggins family hugs and say their goodbyes to each other...but only for now. Sisters, brothers, aunts, uncles, cousins, nieces, nephews and friends realize an upcoming trial will not be easy. It will bring forth new and vivid details of the ruthless and senseless murder of the young man they loved and lost. The new year, 2018, promises to bring yet more heartache and reopen closed and festering wounds to this long suffering, grief-stricken family. Tears will come as the ugly photographs are shown of the torn and mutilated body.

But tonight, the family is not alone. The buried souls and spirits in the church graveyard are now smiling. They will be with them. Justice will prevail. Hopefully, the new year will also bring resolution and peace, something the family has not found for 34 years. They realize justice will be sought when the Georgia summer sun is blazing, when it is hot and humid. But justice is even sweeter after 34 years of wondering, searching, clueless for answers.

Yes. Justice will be sweet and resolution even sweeter.

It has all been so personal for the family.

As the Coggins family drives away…the ghosts lie still underneath their marked and unmarked graves. They know now one of their own has a "proper" grave…a memorial. People, young and old, black and white, now know who Timothy Wayne Coggins is. They know the story. They know the horror.

Oh, if these ghosts could only talk to their loved ones once again. They too would tell the true story. The voices of the unknown ghosts have been silenced only by the tears of their loved ones.

The ghosts and souls lying in the Fuller Chapel United Methodist Church graveyard are ready for the coming year. Timothy Wayne Coggins may have died in a fight for his life. But tomorrow, the beginning of 2018, "Bug," and the other souls of the graveyard will stand up and fight, again for their lives. This time for true justice. It has been a long time, 34 years, but this time these dead souls are unafraid for the world to know who is buried beneath the damp ground in an unknown graveyard.

Tonight.

Tonight, is different.

The silent voices will be heard…for the first time.

With the rising sun a new day and the new year begins.

This is today.

Yesterday is past.

Tomorrow will be a different world.

Chapter 5

Deadly choice at the People's Choice

Friday, October 7, 1983, the People's Choice nightclub

The People's Choice nightclub is located on North Hill Street, about two miles from downtown Griffin. One drives past, "the flats," goes up the hill and on the right is the notorious club. Located in the predominant area where much of the black population of the town once lived, the People's Choice club is rather small. Inside there are tables, a stage area for the music and dancing and of course the bar. You must be twenty-one to enter but identification is seldom checked.

If you wanted to find a watering hole, dance and maybe enjoy some "short term romance," in 1983, the People's Choice club was the place. Another fact, most of the patrons of the People's Choice are black. Whites were welcomed…sort of…well not really. The club wasn't a particularly inviting place unless you could dance and enjoy drinking and shaking and of course…"be romantic."

Timothy Wayne Coggins never had much money, but he could always dig up a little "jingle," to visit the club. Two years over the legal age at 23, Timothy liked the dancing, the liquor, the food and of course the romancing. Coggins could "show off," at the club.

A natural crowd pleaser, Timothy loved people. He always had been friendly, toward everyone, black or white. The social mores of separation did not stop Coggins. He just plain loved anyone…and of course anyone who would love him back. Tim had been warned time and again by his friends and family that being around white people was going to get him in trouble, but he continued to explore his, "unknown."

Jesse Gates, a member of the City of Griffin Police Department, was one in particular who cautioned his friend to, "beware. Remember this kind of stuff (black man dating or dancing with a white woman) might be accepted in Atlanta, but it's not here in Griffin." Jesse knew his community and Timothy well.

It was the last time I saw him

Griffin is a small southern textile town. There had been little racial violence in the town, other than that by the KKK, but things, really had not changed. It was a stage of *tolerance* rather than *acceptance*. And that's just the way it was. Timothy understood the warnings from his friend, his family and Officer Gates, well almost.

Timothy liked the silky white skin of Sue Ellen*. She had met him at the People's Choice club several times to dance. Timothy didn't know if Sue Ellen* would be at the club tonight but his more basic instincts took over and little could stop him from heading north. The problem was he had no money and no transportation. Timothy decided to start walking, but as his good (or bad) fortune would have it, he saw his friend Jesse Gates.

Gates knew the racial climate very well and, "up close." As a City of Griffin Police Officer, he had been required to patrol several of the KKK rallies, parades and gatherings to keep the peace. It was not an assignment he savored.

Gates saw his friend Tim running down the street, near Cabin Creek and Poole Road(s). It was around 10:30 p.m. Gates was not on duty but out in his car to pick up a gallon of milk. "Tim, oh that's Tim," he quickly thought as he saw his young friend running toward him.

Tim arrived at Gates shiny car at the passenger side, out of breath. Gates noticed Tim had something to drink wrapped in a brown paper bag. He didn't know if it was a beer, a Coca-Cola or something else. But Gates knew for a fact he did not allow eating or drinking in his clean car. You see Jesse Gates took pride in his wheels. He knew it, his friends knew it, his fellow officers knew it. Tim also knew the rules and finished his drink and threw the can and wrapper onto the ground.

The off-duty officer asked his friend if he needed a ride. Tim quickly nodded his head yes and hopped into passenger side of the idling car.

Tim asked his friend Jesse if he would take him to the (People's Choice) club. Gates agreed but with hesitation. Gates remembered his friend was all hot over a young white lady. Once again, he cautioned Tim, "If you are going to date a white girl you are going to have to go to Atlanta. Lots of folks here in Griffin do not accept this (inter-racial dating stuff)." But the young Tim could not contain himself. "I've got one of the prettiest (white) girls you would ever want to meet," Coggins smiled.

Gates quickly reminded Tim of their conversation, "Uh-huh. I doubt it. Brother you best be careful. We've had this conversation before."

Gates and Coggins would travel north in the shiny car along North Hill Street toward the People's Choice club. Gates knew the club very well. As a police officer he and others had been there numerous times to break up fights and settle arguments.

As they arrived, Gates knew Tim and knew that he would not have any money and was probably hungry. The officer reached into his pocket and handed his friend five one- dollar bills. "Here. If you find something else (other than food) you know the consequences," Gates shouted to Timothy as he bounded from the car.

Thanks to his police training, Gates would notice something very strange. Two white men and a white woman were waiting outside the club in the parking lot. Tim began to walk toward the three white folks. Jesse Gates would not see Tim go into the club as he drove off, but something in his trained mind, his gut, told him this was the last time he would see his friend alive

New Friends

Little did Gates know the white trio had been waiting for Coggins to arrive at the club for nearly an hour. They knew about Coggins and what he looked like. Coggins somehow had gotten himself up to Sunnyside and Carey's Mobile Home Park one night and had found himself in the arms of a fourteen-year old white girl. How he had gotten out of that place and home he didn't know!

Screaming and hiding in the trailers, Coggins feared the burly white men snarling and hollering. Coggins knew that his emotions had gotten the better of him. Why had he laid down with that young white girl? But he knew he liked it. He really liked it. There had even been talk around town that he had linked up with Frankie Gebhardt's baby sister, Brenda. The talk wasn't true but Gebhardt didn't want to listen.

Tim heard in his head his friends, his family, the police officer, Jesse Gates constantly saying, "Those white girls are gonna get you in trouble." But Tim was 23. He was in love, or was it lust? Timothy was fast. He could get into trouble but also knew he could as quickly talk his way out. Timothy was a charmer. He would simply charm his way out of this again. Timothy Wayne Coggins had been able to do this most of his short life.

As Timothy approached the entry door of the club, one of the men, the slightly taller and thinner of the two, approached him. A conversation quickly ensued with the white man asking Coggins if he knew where he could get some, "candy." Coggins knew the man meant cocaine. Even though he had sold some marijuana and a few pills he found, cocaine was hard to come by. You needed up front money to buy it. And with prices dropping every day during the "Cocaine 80's," Timothy knew it was hard to turn a profit. Timothy smiled and thought, "I'm important. I'm included. A new friend, a white guy about my age. I'm doing him a favor." Coggins and the thin man headed

63

inside the club. The other man, huskier than the first, and woman waited near their gold Mercury Comet automobile.

As they headed inside, several in the tightly packed Friday night crowd turned their heads. It was unusual, but then again not, for a white man to be inside the club. They had seen Timothy several times before dancing with a white woman, but this new, "friend," was a stranger. Out of place among the writhing, steamy, black bodies. Timothy pointed out the black man with the leather hat standing near the bar. He was the one selling drugs.

Getting into the Car

Coggins did as he was told and waited for the white man to come back from the bar. He enjoyed his time smiling and talking with some friends. Tim had forgotten all about being hungry and the money Gates had given him. The white man returned in less than five minutes. A transaction had been made. Coggins and the man began to head back out the door.

Timothy's sister, Telisa, who was two years apart in age from Timothy, had been in the restroom but left just in time to see her brother and the white stranger leaving. "Timothy..." she called out. "TIMOTHY..." she shouted a little louder. Telisa's instincts told her something was not quite right...not quite right. The music was loud, the dancers close, some with their pants unzipped. Telisa tried to move through the tight crowd.

"Timothy...brother...Timothy," she continued to scream.

By the time Telisa reached the front door, a blast of cool October air hit her face. It helped her come to her senses. "Timothy...TIMOTHY," she cried. The sister turned to see a burley white man driving a beaten-up Mercury Comet. A scraggly white woman was in the passenger seat and the stranger who had been inside the club was in the back with her brother. The car quickly turned right, out of the club, and onto North Hill Street leaving a trail of dust in the air. Telisa thought about calling the police but then realized what good would that do? Police came to the People's Choice club many times, especially on Friday nights. Fights, loud arguments, pushing and shoving, and sometimes guns, were all the price you paid to enter Lucifer's liar.

The car rounded the curve heading toward McIntosh Road. This would be the last time anyone from the Coggins family would see their brother and son, Timothy, alive.

No, if you are a black man, you didn't mess with a white woman in the south in 1983.

"Those white bastards ain't coming into my house!"

The car approached McIntosh Road but would immediately double back. Apparently needing gas, the gold Mercury Comet pulled into the gas station across the street from the club. Tim got out and found a phone booth. He would call one of his friends, Samuel Freeman. Freeman would later testify that it was late when Tim called him. Tim told Samuel he was with Frankie Gebhardt. Samuel knew Frankie and knew there was trouble ahead. Freeman would warn Tim, but apparently, "he didn't listen."

Several other people would also testify that they had seen Coggins get out of the car with two white men and a white woman. A couple of dollars of gas was pumped into the tank, everyone loaded up, and the vehicle travelled south on Hill Street, going past the People's Choice club.

Timothy's aunt Linda Morgan Cook lived near town on Collins Street. It was not the best section of town but was adequate for the "after party," being held. After parties were held many times when patrons began leaving the club. Friends would gather and continue their drinking, revelry and hook-ups. It was Friday night and the crowd at her house knew their sins would be absolved by the preacher Sunday in church, that is if they could sober up enough to go. If not, they could go the following Sunday. As the car pulled up, Timothy got out. Cook, a serious looking woman, knew immediately something didn't look exactly right. Three white folks with her nephew in the car. Tim got out and Cook ordered him to stop. She forcefully told Tim, staring at the white passengers that those, "white bastards ain't coming into my house!" Tim knew his aunt and wondered why in the world he had brought his new "friends," to her home. Maybe it was because he was a little high from the cocaine. Maybe he was excited about his new, "friends." Regardless, it was a no-win situation for Tim.

Getting back into the car the foursome pulled out of the driveway. Coggins shouted to his aunt and the several, "after partiers," who were gathered in the driveway they were "going to Sunnyside."

It would be the last time anyone from the Coggins family would see Timothy, until he was identified at the morgue.

A young boy sees the argument

A ten-year old boy, Christopher Joseph Vaughn, who would later be a key witness for the prosecution, had just come out onto the balcony of his home near Carey's

Mobile Home Park. The October evening was cool. The young boy had woken up and could not go back to sleep. Vaughn looked out and saw a Mercury Comet drive up and stop next to one of the trailers. Vaughn's stepfather, Charles Carey, Jr., owned the rough trailer park in Sunnyside. The family lived in an A frame type home next door.

Vaughn knew one the travelers who got out of the car; Frankie Gebhardt. His father and Frankie were friends. But he didn't know the young black man. "Why would a n----- be over there (at the trailer park)," Vaughn thought to himself. Several minutes later a heated argument began, and the young Vaughn heard Gebhardt roar. He didn't know what they were arguing about, but it scared him. It really scared him. He had met Frankie and for a young ten-year-old boy, the burly, thunderous man, was terrifying.

Before Gebhardt, the man and woman entered the car, the ten-year old saw the unknown black man being pushed into the back seat. The car sped out of the mobile home park and turned left onto Wood Road. They would travel a quarter mile and then turn right onto Minter Road, one of the more desolate areas of Spalding County. "Wonder where they are going," the young boy asked himself. Vaughn then shook his shoulders and went back into this bedroom to try and sleep.

Typical Friday night at Carey's Mobile Home Park.

Typical Friday night.

Early Saturday morning, October 8, 1983

The morning sun would shine light on the lifeless body of Timothy Wayne Coggins. It was lying in the underbrush among the lonesome pines. Cows had grazed in these environs for years. There was concern that night when Coggins did not return home. His family thought maybe he had stayed over with some friends. But in actuality, the young black man's life had been taken, far too soon, cut short by this ungodly event. Timothy Wayne Coggins would never enjoy old age, be married, have children or continue to make his "fancy dance moves."

A young life lost to the ages.

Timothy Wayne Coggins had been born, August 29, 1960, under the sign of Virgo. The element for those born on this date is the Earth. "Bug" as he was known to family and friends, was now part of that earth. "Dust to dust," as the Bible notes.

In the Zodiac, numerology, those born on August 29, 1960, have a negative number of eight. It is an "unshakeable and undeniable," sign. Official records list the date of the death of Timothy Wayne Coggins as Sunday, October 9, 1983. This was the date the body was found by the hunters. But those who had been there; the animals, the Evil One, his partners, knew the real date of, "Bug's" death. Timothy Wayne Coggins had been killed just after midnight, in the early morning hours of Saturday, October 8, 1983.

The only person still dancing tonight wasn't Timothy Wayne Coggins...but the Devil.

The Devil never forgot his agreement with Frankie when a younger man had snuck into that meeting with his future KKK brothers. Their language, their hatred, their anger was music to the Devil's ears and his new pledge Franklin George Gebhardt. Frankie had pledged his allegiance to the Devil that night to help him fulfill evil on earth.

The Devil smiled remembering their agreement. Their pact had been fulfilled.

The Devil turned and left the gruesome murder scene looking for his next dance partner.

Chapter 6
Investigation turns cold...
Murder...mailboxes and monkeys

Sunday, October 9, 1983, A beautiful fall day in Georgia

It started like any typical week in Griffin, GA. The Spalding Fair would open. Headlines in the Griffin Daily News announced Griffin Tech, now Southern Crescent Technical College, planned an expansion. A new jail, in which Frankie Gebhardt and Bill Moore would later be incarcerated, began construction, with completion expected in 1984. The national economy, however, was in bad shape. Mortgage lending rates from banks for would be homeowners was 13-13 ½ %. But the jobless rate for Spalding County showed promise, with a 9.3% rate, the "lowest" in seventeen months.

But Sunday, October 9, 1983, was a time to forget troubles. It was a beautiful crisp fall morning. The temperature would hover between 50 and 70 degrees for most of the day. Leaves were falling and beginning to crunch as you walked. Pumpkins began to show up at the front doors of homes, ready to treat children dressed up for Halloween. A lightweight coat or jacket was needed if you were outside, but other than that, the day was perfect. Absolutely perfect.

They say that there is no place on earth like Georgia in the fall. Words are hard to describe exactly what it is like being a southern boy out squirrel hunting with your friends. You know the woods and the well-worn paths. After all you had been here almost since the day you were born.

Yes, it was a perfect day. Absolutely perfect.

That is unless you come across a dead body!

Willard Sanders knew these woods well. He had lived in the area most of his life. Willard and three others; Christopher Vaughn, Charles Carey, Jr., and Keith Garner were in these same woods that beautiful Sunday morning. Some say Barry Sanders and/or Tim Garner were also there, but this was never positively confirmed.

It was about 10:30 a.m. when everyone stopped dead in their tracks. Down the barrel of his small rifle, the 10-year old Vaughn had spotted a larger than normal squirrel which stopped on the branch to strip down a pinecone nut it had just found. The other three men looked and saw the furry animal.
Bap...the rifle fired.

The squirrel fell.

Dead center shot the young boy smiled.

As Sanders walked toward the felled squirrel he came to a sudden stop. "Whoa...there's a body over there," Sanders shouted pointing to the base of the tree. The quartet thought they saw somebody sleeping near "the big old oak tree." As they moved closer it wasn't somebody sleeping...*it was a dead body*. Sanders saw what he later described as a, "n-----man who was dead."

Both the men and young boys were scared. They had never seen a dead body before. The body had cuts and scrapes over most of it. Pants had been pulled down below the ankles. It didn't appear the victim was wearing a shirt or shoes. Whoever it was, was dead. Dead for sure. Sanders turned around and headed back as fast as he could, to make the call...the call to the sheriff.

The four hunters had indeed found the body of a young black man. From the appearance of the scene, it must have been quite a struggle as the victim tried to save his life. There was blood, tire tracks and an empty Jack Daniel's Whiskey bottle 515 feet off the main road.

Dispatch made the call over the radio informing patrolmen that a body had been found in the northern end of the county. A Spalding County Sheriff car thundered north. It turned left onto Minter Road, just below Sunnyside. The deputy got out of the car and a harried Sanders took him to the scene. The other three hunters had barely moved. One of them, probably Vaughn, had thrown up his breakfast nearby.

The deputy was met at the scene by several other sheriff cars, one of them Spalding County Sheriff James C. "Butch" Freeman. This was the second year Freeman had served Spalding County as sheriff. He was elected in November 1980 and would take office in January 1981. One of the deputies began questioning the four men who found the body. The black male body was lying face down in the briars. Conkerberries and grass was matted in his hair. The sheriff noticed numerous stabs over the back of the body. He also noticed a large "X" had been cut into the victim's back. Freeman and the

other deputy turned the body over and were horrified. Maggots and insects had begun to invade the body orifices; the nose, the eyes, the ears, the mouth, the stab wounds on the body. What they saw was a young man…probably in his twenties, about five feet seven or eight inches tall. They had no idea who he was.

They also noticed a small tattoo on his left hand. Whoever this was had a light moustache and goatee. His blue jeans were pulled down to his knees. When the body was turned over, the victim's mouth fell open.

Immediately the deputy noticed that two of his bottom teeth were missing. Other than the missing teeth, it was obvious the victim had taken good are of his teeth.

Investigators arrive

Clint Phillips was the lead investigator assigned to the Coggins murder case. He along with Steve Robinson and Larry Peterson of the GBI Crime Lab, were some of the first people on the scene when Coggins body was found.

It was a hell of a bloody crime scene. One of the worst the young detectives had ever seen.

The trio of investigators noted that the scene was in a rural area, under (electrical) power lines, off a dirt road. This was a cut through from US 19/41 (Highway) to Patterson (Road). Notes were made:

-body of a young black male

-numerous injuries

-slice marks on the neck

-stab wounds in the head

-stab wounds on kneecaps

-stab wounds on the abdomen

-numerous stab wounds and cuts on back of subject

Phillips did notice a peculiar mark on the back of the victim. On the victim's back in the lower part of the abdomen there was an 'X' (carved into the body).

Phillips noted that there were also cut and stab marks on the front of the subject.

Even though the Georgia Bureau of Investigation would arrive later by helicopter, there was not a lot of information shared between the Spalding County Sheriff's Office and the GBI.

Resources of the Spalding County Sheriff's Office were limited. Two to three cases would come into the office each day. Phillips thought to himself that it was too much for the three investigators. And the investigators worked for the sheriff. If he directed you in another direction, you had to go in that direction. The investigators for the local law enforcement were not able to devote all their time to a case, even a murder case. Cases continued to come in and pile up.

Investigator Phillips would note later in his testimony at the trial, "If the sheriff (Butch Freeman) directed you to another case, you would have to do it. Nothing to say despairingly about Sheriff Freeman. He was responsible to all voters in Spalding County." The office of sheriff in

Spalding County is an elected position which is on the ballot every four years.

But the murder case did not take, "top priority in the SCSO. It went cold within three to four months." Phillips did note that, "we estimated the solvability of this case (at that time) to be in the high 80's (80% out of 100%). If we had had the resources Sheriff Dix has today (DNA matching) we would have solved this case. We just didn't have the help (or resources) back then."

Later, when the report was filed, there was no mention of the inner-racial relationships or the white trio at the People's Choice club

It was that same Sunday afternoon, October 9, 1983, when the GBI crime scene team arrived from Atlanta. The Sheriff's Office kept several men on the property to make sure no evidence was disturbed. When GBI Agent Larry Peterson arrived on the scene, the first thing he noticed was the area was very bloody. Peterson thought, "maybe someone helped get rid of some of the evidence and stuff." His observations would later prove to be spot on.

Photographs were taken at the murder scene These would be shown to the jury at the trial. The photographs taken that day would show the decomposing body covered with the red Georgia clay. Pants pulled down past the knees.

Rumors were spread within the community that when found, the victim's penis had been cut off and stuck in his mouth. This was not, however, true or what the investigators found.

It was clear to the GBI that there had been a violent struggle. It was written in investigators notes that the victim had possibly been drug (through the field) and struck in the head with some sort of club or heavy object. Tire tracks at the field were photographed and plaster of Paris casts made.

A rock, a pair of blue jeans, underwear, all covered with blood were found, marked and carefully put into an evidence bag.

But one thing puzzled the detectives, there in the field lay an empty bottle of Jack Daniel's Whiskey. This had not been thrown out on the road by a careless driver, it was too far back. The label on the bottle was too fresh to have been in the woods for any length of time. When one of the lawmen picked the bottle up and smelled, it still had the sweet fragrance of the Tennessee mash therein.

As investigators continued their work, they found four to five lacerations on the face of the victim and several wounds four to six inches deep. A deep stab wound was on the left side of the neck. Several wounds were found on the chest most had likely punctured one or both lungs. Deep gashes were found on the legs and feet. Not breaking the flesh but gashes. Could these be where the victim was drug behind some sort of vehicle in these fields? GBI Agent Peterson noted there were numerous bruises over the body, front and back. Peterson had done enough investigations to realize these were probably defensive marks where the victim had tried to cushion blows from a blunt object.

In his notes Peterson wrote there appeared to be two separate crime scenes. One bloody area where the victim may have been killed. This near the road. The other back from the road where the tire marks had been found. The area, near where the body was found, looked as if some sort of small truck or car had driven around. The grass and dirt and hills looked, "driven over time and again." Peterson wrote in his notebook, "Very violent scene."

The GBI crew collected the evidence and cleaned up. The body carefully laid into a black plastic bag and cautiously loaded onto the crime scene van. It would be taken to Griffin-Spalding County Hospital for an autopsy. The van would drive down Minter Road, then Birdie Road then onto U.S. Highway 19/41. About a mile and a half up the road was Carey's Mobile Home Park in Sunnyside. Gebhardt would not be at home.

Autopsy

Dr. Virgil Williams, Spalding County Coroner, and Warren Tillman, GBI Medical Examiner performed the initial autopsy.

Still not knowing who the victim was, notes were made by Tillman stating the body weighed about 160 pounds. It was bloated and quickly decomposing. Based on his experience Tillman noted that the body had probably been outside anywhere from eighteen to thirty-six hours. This led investigators to conclude that the murder had happened Friday night or early Saturday morning, October 7 or 8, 1983. Maggots and insect activity were prevalent in the body. Tillman noted that maggots can bury themselves into an area about three-eights-of an inch each day.

Starting with the head, Tillman found fine red clay and conkerberries in the hair. Along the body Tillman examined the cuts, lacerations and abrasions. "There were too many to count," he wrote in his report. When the body was cut open, he noted that the lungs were filled with blood, probably from a stab wound. There were lots of bruises on the arms as if the victim was trying to defend himself. At least thirty stab wounds, "so many I quit counting," was listed in the report. Tillman noted in his report that Coggins probably "bled out," within fifteen minutes after being beaten and stabbed.

When Tillman and Dr. Williams examined Coggins clothing, they found a dollar bill inside one of the jean's pockets. It was bloody and stained. This would be labeled and sent to the GBI for analysis. Both Tillman and Williams knew that anything they could have analyzed by what was then primitive forensic equipment, would be valuable to the case. It was all they had to work with at the time. D.N.A. would not be established to determine the origin of blood samples until 1990, and only perfected and accepted years later.

With the autopsy completed, the GBI carefully loaded their evidence back into the van and drove to the crime lab in Atlanta, passing Carey's Mobile Home Park and Sunnyside.

A news article appeared in the Monday, October 10, 1983, issue of the Griffin Daily News describing the murder. Carl Elmore, a reporter with the local newspaper covered the scene that beautiful Sunday afternoon. Elmore wrote, "(Sheriff James) Freeman said law enforcement officials have been unable to identify the victim and are seeking any leads the public can furnish." Elmore went on to describe the victim and the grisly scene. Larry Dale Campbell, an investigator at the scene, told the reporter, "He had been worked over with a knife pretty well. The wounds indicate a struggle occurred. He had defense wounds where he'd thrown up an arm." The article also noted there were, "a number of blood stains were found at the sight," leading investigators to believe the victim had been stabbed to death. Still not knowing who the victim was, Campbell told reporter Elmore, "We don't know if this person was local or a transient. About all we know is that the victim died a violent death." No suspects or motives were known at the time.

The Spalding County Sheriff's investigators went back to crime scene. The area had basically been shut down due to the inquiry Nobody in…nobody out until all evidence had been collected. Clint Phillips and Larry Dale Campbell needed at least four, maybe even six investigators to help them out. Spalding County, while not large in population, is a rather large area. The pair had to go to a scene, gather what they could, and move on. They simply did not have the time to spend to continually analyze a crime scene. After all, this time they had the GBI to help them. And they were the, "big boys, the "glamor guys," from Atlanta."

Campbell identified the remaining evidence, put it into a plastic bag, labeled the bag and took it back with him to evidence storage. He would notify the GBI about what he had found.

Officer Jesse Gates, Timothy's friend also went to the scene of the crime, on his own. Because of his training, Gates wanted to, "walk the field. See if I could connect any evidence, (to the crime)." Gates would later be told to, "stop (his) personal investigation," when the GBI was brought in. "The case closed fairly quickly," Gates would testify later. "There was not a lot of sharing of information."

By Tuesday, October 11, 1983, Coggins body had been identified. A grieving family had been notified; a funeral planned. An article written by Elmore in the Griffin Daily News said the GBI had identified the body, "through crime lab fingerprints and other data gathered during an investigation." Elmore reported that Coggins lived at 635 East Solomon Street in Griffin and was 23 years old. Family was being notified. Sheriff Freeman was quoted as saying, "We'll follow the trail to wherever it leads."

Sadly, the Thursday, October 13, 1983, issue of the Griffin Daily News would announce the obituary of Timothy Wayne Coggins. "Funeral services for Mr. Timothy Wayne Coggins will be Friday, October 14, 1983 in the Fuller Chapel United Methodist Church in Zebulon. The Rev. Jeremiah Lyons will officiate. Burial will be in the church cemetery.

"Survivors include his mother, Mrs. Viola Dorsey; father Marshall Lawrence; stepfather Robert Lee Dorsey; four sisters, Mrs. Peggy Richard, Miss Harriette Coggins, Miss Telisa Coggins and Miss Jacqueline Coggins, all of Griffin; three brothers, Eugene Coggins, Dwayne Coggins, both of Griffin and Ramon Coggins of Atlanta; grandparents Mr. and Mrs. Robert Lawrence of Milner, eight aunts, eight uncles, nieces and nephews.

"Friends may visit the family at 635 E. Solomon St. McDowell Funeral Home is in charge of plans."

As the family buried Timothy that October day, they remembered a loving son, brother grandchild, nephew and friend. He was much like his stepfather the family remembered He could fix everything and anything. He had a strong work ethic. He took care of his family. If they wanted to go anywhere, "Bug" would walk with them. Every time he left his home, he would tell his mother he loved her and gave her a kiss. Even though she had several other sons and daughters, Viola would miss that sweet kiss from her son Timothy.

Viola would die in 2016. Timothy's stepfather, Robert Lee would die in 2017.

Leads in the case would slowly dry up. The trail went cold. Even the most sensitive bloodhound's nose could not sniff out, "who done it."

No one imagined at the time it would take over 34 years to solve the murder.

Scraggly, skanky white woman

A few weeks after the funeral, a scraggly skanky white woman showed up at the Spalding County Sheriff's Office. The woman looked tired and gaunt. Co-conspirator Ruth Elizabeth "Mitzie" Guy had gone to talk to sheriff deputies after Frankie had beaten her, both on October 21, and again three days later, on October 24, 1983. There were bruises on her arms. Her right eye was black with red marks around the eyelids and socket. She was tired of his rage, his anger, his drinking, the beatings but most of all was fearful of what she had witnessed her one-time lover had done. Angry before, it seemed that Gebhardt had gotten even angrier and madder, if that was possible. He was also drinking almost all day and night. Ruth Guy feared for her life. She knew what her, "old man," was capable of. He had bragged many times at parties about the killing.

Guy wanted someone to talk to about the incident. When asked by deputies, "Who beat you up?" the answer was a name the lawmen knew well, "Frankie Gebhardt," Guy answered quickly. Larry Dale Campbell and Clint Phillips had interviewed a couple of pulp-wooders working the area of the murder a couple of days back. Gebhardt, one of the pulp-wooders, gave solid answers and the investigators didn't think anything else about it. Ruth Guy skirted in and out evading direct questions about the murder. She knew that if the investigation got into full swing, she would become a prime suspect. Guy did not want to serve jail time for the murder of a "n-----."

Ruth Elizabeth "Mitzie" Guy would soon leave not only Griffin and Spalding County but also the State of Georgia. Perhaps she wanted to get away from the beatings she suffered from Gebhardt. Perhaps she felt the "cold case," would soon be solved and name her as a direct suspect and link to the murder. Before she left Guy purchased some snacks from the Easy Shop supermarket in Experiment, using one of the blood-stained dollars she took off Coggins dead body found in his blue jeans pocket. She knew what was coming.

Ruth knew it was time to, "get the hell out of Dodge."

She would then simply disappear.

Guy was never heard from again nor was she arrested for her part in the crime. She would die a lonely, broken woman, one of the few who knew the truth from that awful dark night. Ruth Elizabeth "Mitzie" Guy took with her the nightmares of a younger woman cheering her lover on at that sordid murder scene.

Monday, November 1, 1983

The black community in Griffin and Spalding County began to ask Sheriff Freeman when the case would be solved, and suspects brought to justice. Freeman did not have an answer. He knew that he had only so many men and so many resources to do real factfinding work. Freeman had to depend on the GBI to do the detective work on this case and he knew they were not sharing much of anything they had discovered. The case was going nowhere fast. Freeman had to do something.

An idea popped into his head. Why not assign Oscar Jordan to the case? He could help be a sort of liaison between the sheriff's department and the black community. Jordan was the perfect candidate. He was a patrol officer for the department and knew the community very well.

In 1983, Oscar Jordan was a uniformed patrol officer with the Spalding County Sheriff's Office. He and the Coggins family lived down the street from each other. They knew each other but not very well. Jordan knew that the black community was not talking to the GBI or the Spalding County Sheriff's office. He knew it was 1983 and they were still scared. Officer Jordan knew that the (Ku Klux) Klan activity was still strong in Spalding County. He also knew if the word got out someone from the black community had answers to the case, they too might be found stabbed to death in the middle of nowhere. Jordan had even been asked to identify the body at the hospital autopsy but could not due to decomposition.

As he patrolled the area, Officer Jordan came up with some clues, bits of information. He knew the clientele of the People's Choice club. He knew that some things happened down there that were not, "for the record." Jordan reported this information and what he had found both to the sheriff investigators and to the GBI, but would later testify that he, "really did not know if things were being followed up or not. Not a lot of information was being shared back and forth (between the Spalding County Sheriff and the GBI)."

Wednesday, December 15, 1983

It was ten days before Christmas. The family would look back years later and realize the weeks had turned into months and months had turned into years. And there was still no suspect in the murder of their loved one, Timothy Wayne Coggins. Little was published, known or discovered about this murder. The family became disheartened. It was the first Christmas "Bug," would not be with them. It was going to be a sad and lonely Christmas at the Dorsey-Coggins household.

Sheriff Freeman continued to remind everyone his office had limited resources. They would have to concentrate on things at hand. Prominent citizens of the community had recently had their mailboxes vandalized and blown up with firecrackers. Always thinking of his political consequences, Freeman knew he would be facing reelection in the coming year, 1984. Sheriff James C. "Butch" Freeman knew who he had to answer to, and it was *not* the black community. The Spalding County Sheriff had to move on. There were other, "more important," things to solve.

This was, after all, the murder of, "just another black man."

The case would stay cold for another thirty-four years.

In fact, the case was so cold it was said by investigators it was, "cold enough to freeze the balls off a brass monkey."

Chapter 7
The "wild and crazy party"

Inflict as much harm and damage as possible

This had been a crime of *passion*. The accused killer, unknown by law enforcement officials at the time, wanted to kill Timothy Wayne Coggins and, "kill him good." Law enforcement records show that when a gun is used in a crime, many times the act is impassioned. The victim and perpetrator seldom know each other. But when a person is unmercifully stabbed, body mutilated by dragging it through pastureland as was Coggins, the killer means to inflict as much harm and damage as they possibly can to the victim.

Not only did Timothy Coggins die because he had, "danced with a white woman," but his alleged sexual activity with alleged white women drove Gebhardt into a blind rage. He wanted to inflict harm, as much as he could, but he also wanted to remind the Coggins family and the entire black community, he was in charge. His word was the law. He was above society's rules and morals.

The bloody shirt and dog

The relentless harassment continued toward the community and toward the Coggins family. The Sunnyside thug was not through. "As much harm and damage as possible."

Shortly after the family had buried their own in an unmarked grave at Fuller Chapel United Methodist Church, unusual things, strange things, began to happen. Phone calls to the family. No one there. A sudden hang up and the buzzing sound of a disconnected line. Cars driving slowly by their East Solomon Street home, stopping, then speeding off.

Timothy's stepfather, Robert Lee Dorsey drove a school bus. According to records and reports he was one of the best drivers the school system employed. Back at that time, school bus drivers usually parked their assigned school buses near to where they lived, simply because they could get out early and get back quicker from their appointed routes.

One early morning Robert Lee left his house to go crank his bus to get it warm for his students. He loved his students and wanted to take care of them as best he could. Robert Lee would open the door and gasp. A bloody shirt lying in the entry way. "Who could have done this horrible thing," Dorsey wondered. Then he saw the note. "You're NEXT!!!" It left no doubt of the message or the intent. It was meant to scare his already heartbroken family. Hadn't they suffered enough at the hands of these monsters? Why wasn't the sheriff doing more to solve the crime? Wasn't the GBI involved? Dorsey knew what he had to do. Contact Sheriff Deputy Oscar Jordan.

A few weeks later the horror would be multiplied on the bereaved family.

Sister Telisa sat up in bed, fully awake after the horrifying howl outside her bedroom window. Brothers Eugene and Raymon had heard the yelp as well. As the trio gathered and looked out into the murky night. They saw one...no two...dark objects lying in the grass outside their door. Fearful it might be another body the brothers grabbed a flashlight. By now the entire family was awake. Carefully they shined the beam onto the object and saw a large dog, a German Shepard type dog. Further examination with the flashlight showed a detached dog head, blood everywhere. As the brothers crept toward the mangled body of the dog, another note was found. Again, it read, "You're NEXT!"

It was as if the sins of Job had befallen the family. There seemed to be no way out of the continued misery and reminders of their lost Timothy.

Bragging about the murder

Gebhardt and his murderous thugs, were not ones to forgive or forget. Gebhardt began to brag about the murder. With the bragging also came threats, mostly from Frankie, about what would happen if someone crossed him. Then there were the parties. The constant drinking, snorting and fornicating at Carey Mobile Home Park parties. They were wild, for most of the civilized world. But again, this was the norm at Carey's.

Christopher Vaughn attended one of these parties with his stepfather, Charles Carey, Jr. Christopher had tagged along to be with other children. Vaughn heard Gebhardt brag that they had, "killed a man…him and Bill Moore." Frankie was always throwing Moore's name into the mix. He still wanted to get back Moore for some reason. Gebhardt didn't seem to be ashamed of the crime but was rather boastful. Frankie was smart enough, not to relate where or who had been killed. That is until Frankie drank a little and snorted (cocaine) a little more. The young boy also heard the older Gebhardt brag about how they had, "used a chain to wrap around (Coggins) ankles," and used a, "truck to drag the body up and down the field." The 10-year old Vaughn didn't know what to think, or even in the story was true. But he did know that he feared the man his stepfather called his, "friend."

Frankie was a mean drunk. When he drank, he also got angry and violent! When questioned by one of the party goers about the murder, Frankie became visibly upset. The rage showed in his face. "I'll kill you like just I killed that n-----," Frankie boomed. The fact was, Franklin George Gebhardt nor his posse liked blacks.

The story might change with the bragging; one-time Frankie had stabbed Coggins, another Bill had stabbed Coggins, but the fact would never change. Frankie Gebhardt was proud he had killed another human being, especially a black man. And even prouder he had seemingly gotten away with it.

Gebhardt wanted to prove that he was superior. He kept on bragging about, how he was, "not to be messed with." Frankie thought he was without peer. The words and stories he began to share with his cohorts and fellow revilers grew bolder with each tale. There was little fear from Gebhardt that his crimes would be discovered, much less prosecuted by an outgoing sheriff. After all, he was Frankie Gebhardt. He was like a king, a kind of god in these parts of Spalding County. He was untouchable and without sin or fault. His word, not the sheriff's, was the law.

Another young party participant that night was Charles Lloyd Sturgill. Sturgill was another of the, "rogue's gallery," of witnesses the prosecution had lined up to testify in the trial 34 years later. Sturgill is currently serving time in a federal penitentiary in Florida for dealing and distributing meth. When arrested Sturgill had 72 pounds (yes pounds) of meth on him ready for distribution.

Sturgill and his family had moved into Carey's Mobile Home Park in 1984 when he was 15 years old. "It was not a very good place," Sturgill recollected. "It was prominently white."

Sturgill would remember the parties and life Gebhardt led in Sunnyside. "Lots of folks in the Sunnyside area were afraid of him (Gebhardt). I was too. But I'm not now."

Sturgill would recall one time when, "Frankie had gotten into an argument with Pee-Wee (Howard). Frankie let me drive his car. (On the way) The police pulled me over for no driver's license." The car, Frankie's car, was impounded. When Sturgill got back home (to Carey's), "Frankie saw me and asked, 'where's my f---ing car?' I told him it was impounded. Frankie then told me 'You got 'til 6 p.m. tonight (to get the car back). Or the same thing that happened to that n----- is going to happen to you.' I knew he was serious."

On another occasion Sturgill related that, "We were going to the liquor store. On the way back, Frankie stopped and put me out. Frankie got out and we were walking down a dirt road and Frankie pointed to an area, 'That's where I stabbed that n-----.' I was scared."

Sturgill would conclude, "It was widely known in Sunnyside that Frankie openly bragged about the murder. He would say it around other people…many times."

Another of the revilers that evening was one of Frankie's long time, closest friends, Willard Sanders. Sanders, who would later be well known to local law enforcement officers as well as the penal system of Georgia, had lived in the area most of his life. He and Frankie Gebhardt had been friends since they were about six years old.

Sanders, known of as a, "habitual violator," had been one of the men and boys who had found Coggins dead body while squirrel hunting that Sunday morning. As Sanders bragged, Gebhardt and he were, "drinking buddies. Yeah, Frankie and me has drunk a lot of beer (together).

I like beer. It's pretty good when it's hot. (I suppose), Frankie and me have drunk enough beer to float a battleship!"

When he spotted Willard at the party, Frankie strutted directly toward his friend and asked him to sit down with him, so they could talk in private. Frankie asked Willard, "Did you find the body?" Sanders acknowledged yes; he had found Coggins body. Gebhardt would then go on to tell they had, "put a log chain on the body and drug him and killed him." Gebhardt would share "the n----- had been stabbed numerous times. It was good to see him die," Gebhardt smiled at his old friend.

Sanders was not surprised. He knew his buddy well and that he had been involved with the KKK. He also knew his friend hated "n------." But Sanders, wondered, even up until the day he would testify, why?

The party

Robert Eugene Smith, who would later be yet another of the "rogue's gallery," of prosecution witnesses, attended a party at Carey's when he and his father were doing some vinyl siding work in Griffin in late 1983. They had driven to the Spalding County area from Alta, GA. Smith's father hired both Gebhardt and Moore to help him take down some trees on property he had just purchased. Bill Moore's brother, Rodney invited Smith to come to one of the parties in Sunnyside.

The party began the usual way with cans of beer consumed at an alarming rate to others, but normal to this group. The Friday weekly paychecks helped stock the coolers. "The devil's candy," was snorted followed with chugs of Jack Daniels Whiskey, passed from one hero to another with only a wipe of a dirty hand before consumption. What seemed to start as a normal get together for the seasoned veterans morphed into a drunken orgy.

Robert Eugene Smith would remember that it was a pretty violent party at Carey's Mobile Home Park. "These guys were crazy. There was mushroom tea, different liquors, marijuana. Any type of drug, you name it, was there."

Revilers would stagger from one trailer to another, peering inside to see tattered couches littered with bare chested men fondling bare chested women. Even the younger women, and most of the men, looked to be well past their prime. It was not the "first rodeo," for anyone there. The dalliance would stop only momentarily to chug a little more of their, "black jack," with the word "black" said in positive defiance. Joints were passed and smoked until the tips burned the fingers of the last, "doobie brother." Snorts heard, and noses wiped. If the action got heated, as it often did, bedrooms were close by to consume the final acts of the animal barbarism.

One particular, "wild, crazy party," Smith remembered involved a baby calf.

Smith would share that the group of revilers would butcher a baby calf they found in the fields near the trailer park. It was a gruesome scene as the baby calf was slaughtered.

Frankie knew a thing or two about hunting and knew how to butcher animals for meat. He would freeze the meat and eat most of it through the winter, which was fast approaching. Although he was nowhere an expert, he got the job done.

Gebhardt smiled at the group of men. They had done what they were told.

You stayed until Frankie was through. You stayed until he said it was time to go or dismissed you. Frankie had chains, knives and chain saws. He knew how to do something to you. How to mess you up real bad. Something you would remember…forever.

With his black, soulless, evil eyes, Frankie stared and smiled at the men and told them killing wasn't so bad.

Everyone nodded yes.

They understood.

Frankie Gebhardt ruled the dark side of Sunnyside. He and his buddies had free run and terrorized the area for years. He was the Godfather if you will. Homage was paid to Frankie. The ring was kissed. The orders carried out. Like it or not, you did what Frankie Gebhardt said to do. You didn't disobey Frankie when he told you to do something. The men, and women at the party knew Frankie meant business and was not to be messed with, especially when he was drunk and high.

 Without a doubt, everyone understood Franklin George Gebhardt that night at the, "wild, crazy party."

++++++++

Years later, in 2016, a year before he was arrested, Gebhardt was still boasting about the murder. Robert Eugene Smith, who was temporarily out of prison was with Gebhardt once again, but this time at his home on Patterson Road. Everyone was still drinking. But these days the partying was a little less "crazy," than in years past. Smith asked (Gebhardt) if he remembered the party at Carey's Mobile Home Park and how he was bragging about killing (Coggins). Frankie quickly answered, "hey, we don't put up with that kind of shit, black and white. You know how we deal with that kind of stuff." Smith would testify that Gebhardt would never share with him, "how he killed Coggins," but he did say why.

"For messing with a white girl."

++++++++

Thirty-four years later you still didn't mess with the boss. Everyone still understood who was in charge in Sunnyside. You don't mess with Franklin George Gebhardt.

Chapter 8

The things I wish I hadn't seen…the things I wish I hadn't done

What shapes a 10-year old boy?

Who knows what shapes the mind of a young boy, especially the mind of a young 10-year old boy?

Could it have been a heated argument between two white men and a black man he witnessed that cool October night outside his bedroom balcony?

Anyone, young or old, that comes upon a dead, mutilated, maggot infested body in the middle of the woods would have traumatic nightmares.

Perhaps the ears of a young boy, who is in his formative years, could be affected when he heard a friend of his stepfather brag about, "killing a n-----."

Thinking this was accepted behavior from adults could have shaped the man the 10-year old boy was yet to be.

Who knows why Christopher Joseph Vaughn was in and out of trouble with the law by the time he reached his early 20's, a short ten years after he had found Coggins' body?

Regardless, Vaughn's first recorded brush with the law occurred when he was charged with forgery. The year is unknown. Another two marks on his record were for theft by taking, again year unknown. By the time Christopher Joseph Vaughn turned twenty-five years old, he had three arrests. In 1998 he was charged and sentenced, again for four counts of forgery. When he turned twenty-six, Vaughn was arrested a second time for theft by taking. He then broke into and entered a vehicle in 1999 and by 2001, his crime involved theft by deception.

But the most repulsive acts Vaughn would commit were between 2004 and 2006. He was arrested, charged and sentenced for, "Child Molestation and Sex Exploitation of a Child," Case number 599314 shows Vaughn sentenced to fifty years in prison. He was thirty-one years old. Vaughn is eligible for parole on October 14, 2054. He will be eighty-one years old if released then. Any act of child molestation or exploitation is disgusting, but Vaughn's case was especially nauseating. Freedom was not soon to come to this monster.

Who knows what motivated Vaughn to begin to talk with the GBI about the murder? Perhaps Vaughn doesn't even know. Maybe he realized 2054 is a long time off. Maybe, just maybe, he could get some early release time for any facts or discussion he could provide the agents. It was worth a chance. Vaughn would begin telling the GBI the tale of what he knew about the 1983 murder in 2005.

He would meet with the agency again three times before disclosing that he had heard Gebhardt admit to the crime. Vaughn's and Gebhardt's paths had crossed several times within the penal system. This was 2017. Vaughn had been in jail for over a decade. Perhaps GBI agent, Jared Coleman would listen to him with a fresh ear and he could share what he knew about the murder.

It was April 2017, and the prosecution had been receiving tips about the 34-year old murder of a black man at the hands of two Sunnyside thugs. Christopher Joseph Vaughn would be considered a, "key witness," in the murder case. A "shaky witness," but key witness, nonetheless. The prosecution and GBI wanted to solve this cold murder case and Vaughn was the best they had. At this point it was all they had. It was fourth down and a long way to score the winning touchdown. This was what worried them.

The year 2016 and early 2017

The Georgia Bureau of Investigation reexamines cold cases twice a year to see if there are any new clues, changes or items that need to be checked out. In 2016 Georgia Bureau of Investigation Special Agent Jared Coleman was assigned to review the October 1983 murder case of Timothy Wayne Coggins. GBI Agent

Robert DeVane, who retired, assigned Coleman the case. Little did Coleman know that he would be involved in one of the coldest murder cases that had ever been recorded in Georgia, if not the United States. The, "unsolvable case," however, would soon be solved.

GBI Special Agent Jared Coleman works near Columbus, in Midland, GA, in the regional GBI office. This office handles cases from 13 surrounding Georgia counties, of which Spalding is one.

The GBI Special Agent began his police work while still enrolled in at the University of North Georgia in Dahlonega. Coleman would attend school during the day, work as a policeman with Gwinnett County at night (10 p.m. until 7 a.m. shift), then do it all over again. He laughs and remembers that many times he would catch a few, "hours of sleep in the police station before his shift. It was tough, but it was something I wanted to do," Coleman smiled. He joined the GBI in 2015.

By the time 2017 rolled around Coleman had been reviewing the Coggins murder for several months. He kept seeing a name, Christopher Joseph Vaughn, come up, time and again. Vaughn had been questioned by the GBI and law enforcement in 2007, 2008, 2015 and 2017 about the cold case. Coleman had read the summary –

statements and interview transcripts with Vaughn by both GBI agents Daniel Green and Samuel Baity. Green and Baity would later become the only two witnesses the defense team would call to the stand during the trial.

With hesitation and lack of confidence in the information Vaughn claimed, Coleman remembered he pledged to investigate any new leads that might come about in the Coggins "cold case," murder. Even as unreliable as Vaughn may be, he did have information. What Coleman would learn that day got the wheels in motion. Perhaps he could get Vaughn in a cell with Gebhardt and maybe…just maybe Gebhardt would confess to the murder on tape.

Entering the lion's den

A wire to record a conversation with a suspect requires approval from a judge. One of the four Spalding County Superior Court judges at the time, Judge Scott Ballard, approved the order. This would allow law enforcement to put a wire on Vaughn's body and have him in the same Spalding County Jail cell with Franklin George Gebhardt.

Arrangements were made to move Vaughn into the Spalding County Detention Center from his jail cell at the Riverbend Correctional Facility in Milledgeville, GA. Gebhardt was already in the Spalding County jail for a charge of "Sexual Battery," the thirty-fourth charge of his criminal career.

Plans called for the investigative team to have Vaughn enter the cell with Gebhardt first. They would then bring Vaughn back out to debrief and send him in back into the cell one more time, again debriefing at the end. At that point investigators planned to bring Frankie out and ask him questions while recording the answers. Plans were set. All systems, GO.

Captain Mike Morris is one of Spalding County's top investigators. He planned the wire with GBI Special Agent Coleman. Morris grew up in Griffin and knows his community having served in both the Griffin Police Department (uniformed traffic patrol) and the Spalding County Sheriff's Office (narcotics and criminal investigator). Morris is one of Sheriff Dix's top, "go to men." Captain Morris has received numerous commendations and awards during his career.

Both Morris and Coleman were anxious about the meeting between Gebhardt and Vaughn.

On Thursday, April 27, 2017, at 10:42 a.m., Christopher Joseph Vaughn, with a wire recording device taped to his body, was moved into a cell with Franklin George Gebhardt. The audio transcript reveals the jail cell cold steel door slamming shut and locking. GBI Special Agent Jared Coleman and Captain Mike Morris along with Lt. Todd Harris of the Spalding County Sheriff Department were waiting in another room listening.

Gebhardt quickly asked Vaughn as he was led into the cell, "What's all this about?"

Vaughn replied, "I guess same shit as yesterday."

Gebhardt had gained a lot of weight during his prison stay, as much as 40-50 pounds. He is also hard of hearing. During much of the time he was with Vaughn, Gebhardt kept asking, "Huh," appearing not to understand or hear the question Vaughn was asking. Vaughn would have to repeat himself time after time after time.

Gebhardt, "I'm fixing to raise hell, you watch." Gebhardt then went to the toilet in the cell, peed and flushed.

Gebhardt, "You know what this is for?"

Vaughn, "Same shit, different day. Same shit, different day."

When Vaughn asked Gebhardt if he had taken a lie detector test, Gebhardt answered, "Nah."

Vaughn then suggested Gebhardt call his sister, Sandra
Bunn his protector.

Vaughn, "You call your sister yet?"

Gebhardt, "Uh-huh. I'm telling her to call me. I'm telling
her to call me."

Vaughn replied, "Well they should. This is the first time in
30 years they talked to you about this thing?"

"Damn right," Gebhardt replied.

The duo began talking about lunch and how the jailers
would bring their lunch to them.

Vaughn remembered what he was there to do and began
again to ask Gebhardt about the suspected murder.

Vaughn, "Thirty years…34 years and they want to drag
this shit back up."

Gebhardt replied, "Yeah. All they doing is pissing in the
wind. That's all they doing is pissing in the wind.
(Unintelligible) going to put a lawsuit on their ass. Yep,
that's what I'm going to do."

At this point on the tape, Gebhardt could be heard
tapping his foot very quickly on the floor, clearly getting
agitated with the situation and Vaughn's questions.

Vaughn and Gebhardt began discussing the situation
again.

Gebhardt, "I don't know what the f---'s going on."

Vaughn, "I told you yesterday what they were investigating."

Gebhardt, "I don't know why they (are) investigating me."

Vaughn, "They think you done it."

Gebhardt, "They dead ass wrong. They dead ass wrong!"

Vaughn, "At least, you know something about it they think. One of the two. They got to know something, think something."

Gebhardt, "I don't know nothing about it."

Vaughn, "They been f---ing with you forever. They been investigating you forever, Frankie."

Gebhardt, "I don't know a damn thing. About the only thing I can tell them…(unintelligible)."

Vaughn, "I mean they got to have something new they talking to all us."

Gebhardt, "I don't reckon, they ain't got shit on me. Ain't got shit on me. I'm gonna tell them too. Watch. They dead ass wrong, can't put that shit on me. Watch me."

Vaughn then told Gebhardt, "They like your (unintelligible) for some reason. You say they were investigating you for five years last time?"

Gebhardt, "Yeah."

Vaughn, "I don't know which one they gonna interview first. It's them same investigators."

At this point a jailer came toward the cell. They pointed toward Vaughn and told him, "We're going to go down this way."

With that they unlocked the cell, showed Vaughn the way out and locked Gebhardt behind in his cell. The jailer showed Vaughn to another room where Agent Coleman and Morris were sitting.

Doritos and orange hands

Coleman, "Have a seat. Keep in mind that your recording device is still on."

Vaughn, "Yeah. I got a little red light there. I didn't notice it until I threw my leg up right there and I was like ah f---."

Coleman, "What's he saying?"

Vaughn, "He's telling me that...uh...he's gonna tell y'all that he'd take a lie detector test and that you're barking up the wrong tree. He ain't really saying anything. I told him that I guess they gonna to talk to both of us. So, we'll see what goes on when y'all talk to him about it."

Coleman, "What else is he saying?"

Vaughn, "He says he's just…he says he can barely f---ing remember us finding him (the body of Coggins). So…well that's what he's saying today, but that ain't what he was saying yesterday."

Coleman, "Uh-huh. What was he saying yesterday?"

Vaughn, "He was talking about it casually like this, you know what I mean?

Coleman, "Uh-huh. What else was he asking you?"

Vaughn, "He just asked me if I had been up there the whole time and if I'd seen anybody. I said, nah I hadn't seen anybody yet. I'm just sitting here waiting on f---ing them to decide what they're going to do."

Vaughn had been complaining how cold and nervous he was. Coleman assured him that it was ok and passed him a Coca-Cola and a bag of Doritos.

Vaughn, "Appreciate it."

Coleman, "So what did you say when y'all…what did he say when you first got in the cell.

Vaughn, "He said you (Vaughn) been up here the whole time? I said yeah. He said, you ain't seen nobody. I said, nah. I said I guess it's about the same shit as yesterday. I said at least they maybe going to talk to the both of us and get it over with."

Coleman, "Did he say anything as far as whether or not he was going to talk to us?"

Vaughn, "Uh-huh."

Coleman, "He said he would?"
Vaughn, "He (Gebhardt) said he's gonna…he said he has some stuff he was going to tell y'all because y'all barking up the wrong tree and he's gonna sue y'all when this got through."

Vaughn would continue, "I said they don't just do that out of the blue. So (unintelligible) do it, you know what I mean.

Captain Mike Morris then asked Vaughn, "What was he saying when he was being so animated? He leaned up and he had his hands going and he was…"

Vaughn, "He was talking about I don't even…he was talking about he didn't remember it. He said that I barely remember y'all finding him (Coggins body). But we were back there yesterday and talking about it and he (was) just talking like it was yesterday."

Coleman, "What was he saying then (the day before)?"

Vaughn, "He was talking about how it was…yeah he was telling me who all was there. You know what I mean?"

Coleman, "Uh-huh."

Vaughn, "If you can't remember it…barely remember it then you wouldn't remember everybody that was (there)."

Harris then asked Vaughn, "Did you tell him that? It's funny you was talking about it yesterday and now…?"

Vaughn, "Nah. I was just starting, you know what I mean?"

Coleman, "Who did he say was all there yesterday (when Coggins body was found)."

Vaughn, "Me. My dad (Charles Carey, Jr.), Barry Sanders and Willard Garner (perhaps meaning Willard Sanders), and Keith Garner. Keith's Garner's dead now so y'all can't talk to him. He's passed away. I don't know if you knew that or not?"

Questions then were asked of Vaughn if these were the Garners that lived on Old Atlanta Road, the road that leads past Sunnyside.

Vaughn, "Last time I left, they was living out there around 155 (Highway 155 which leads from Griffin to McDonough)? I mean they (the Garners) move. Some of them ain't got no money. They don't own no properties so they move whenever the hell they can. I'm giving it a shot guys! I don't know if it's going to work but…"

Coleman then reassured Vaughn that everything was alright. He then asked Vaughn if he had heard what was being discussed in the adjacent cell when he was talking to Gebhardt.

Vaughn, "They was talking about…oh…he's snitching. I'm not worried about it. Maybe you could bring up…I don't know if you'd want to or not…bring up the knife in the well."

After the officers agreed Vaughn suggested, "Somebody…somebody might have told y'all (about the knife in the well). You've heard it from other sources or something. And I'm mistaken yesterday. I apologize. It wasn't…uh…kin folks that have the truck. It was Bill Moore's kin folks. He's (Gebhardt) wondering why Bill hasn't been investigated for this? He actually thinks Bill might have been talking to (the officers). I don't know if y'all can use that to your advantage either. Think of anything (Captain) Morris? Can you think of anything?"

Captain Morris, "What do you think would happen when you…when you go back over there if you tell him (Gebhardt) that you told us about him saying that he threw the knife in the well and that…him admitting that he killed him (Coggins) and you confront him with that? I mean here's the thing, if you and I were in a room, ok? And I said that I shot Agent Coleman, and I told you that, there's no way of getting around that. There's no way I can ever take that back. There's no way I can erase that from your mind, ok? Oh, he has said those things. So, if you go over there, and tell him exactly what you've told Agent Coleman, and you confront him with that, and you say I was honest, I told him that you threw the knife in the well. I told him that you've killed, or you said you've killed him. I'm honest with them. I'm not getting in any trouble, and I'm sure not going to jail for giving false statements of whatever the case may be. What do you think his reaction to that would be?"

Vaughn, "He (Gebhardt) has an explosive temper, so I don't know if it would be better to wait until after you talk to him or…"

Agent Coleman, "I think it would be a better idea to do that now when we get done here. The reason I say that is because either he is going to flat out deny it or he's got to acknowledge that he's made the statements in the past."

Vaughn, "Well, if you do it that way then I won't be able to go back in there with him after you get done talking to him. So that eliminates that part. You see what I am saying?"

Captain Morris, "So are you saying that it would be better to not have that conversation now? Pull him out and then confront him with the facts that you just told us that and then put him back in there with you? For him to say what you told them that?"

Vaughn, visibly scared with the possibility of the confrontation with Gebhardt's anger said, "I don't know how y'all want to do that."

Captain Morris, "I'm asking you."

Lt. Todd Harris to Coleman and Morris, "What if we let him...what if we take Chris back, bring him (Gebhardt) out, talk and try to interview him, when he don't say nothing, then put him back in there. Then he could say it and then we can pull Chris out and take him back there and you pull him back in there. What about that?"

Captain Morris, "The only thing about that is if he decides to invoke his right to an attorney."

+++++++

At this point, Gebhardt had only been charged with the crime of sexual battery for which he was awaiting a trial. He had not been charged with the murder of Timothy Wayne Coggins. His Miranda rights had been read to him for the previous arrest. It was later determined by the court, that the Miranda rights need not be read to

Gebhardt at this point since he had not been charged with the murder.

+++++++

Harris, "That's true."

Vaughn then began to explore other options with the officers. "Now you got other options. You could do this. Y'all could talk to him. I don't know what your time frame on this. You talk to him and if we don't get anything useful today, bug a room. I'll move in with him back there and see if we can work something out. See if we can get him talking."

Agent Coleman quickly spoke up, "I think this is a one-shot deal man."

Vaughn, "I know him (Gebhardt)...so I know he's got an explosive temper. But if you tell him before, if I saw something like that before he comes in here and talk to y'all. He said he may lawyer up. Then you're dead."

Agent Coleman, "What we want to know is what he...what his response to you is going to be more so than what he's going to tell us. Because I've already got him in lies in his original interview. He said that he didn't know Tim Coggins. You said that you've seen them associating with Tim Coggins. Other people have."

Vaughn, "Hell people have...I can't even remember his name. There was another guy up there talking with me one time about it. We were talking about it. And he knew about it and he was telling me some people that was down in Broadway Groceries when that's where Coggins was supposedly picked up. And they seen him with (them). So...I mean y'all tell me how you want to work it and I'll work it. You know what I'm saying."

The officers would discuss the plan amongst themselves at this point.

Vaughn spoke up again, "But we do it to where I say something about that, that's all bets off because he's probably not going to talk to me anymore and he's gone...he's going to be ill. He's probably going to swing on me. So, I will kill that whole operation. You see what I'm saying? I won't be able to go back in there with him."

Lt. Harris, "He's going to know you ratted him when you go back in there smelling like Doritos. He's going to know you did something."

Captain Morris, "You just got to wipe those fingers off and get rid of all that orange cheese off them.

Lt. Harris, "You gonna have to (go) in that bathroom and wash (your) mouth out with water (too)."

Vaughn informed the officers that the prison had Doritos available. "Matter of fact, there is a bag in my room."

The officers continued to discuss the plan and options of putting him back in the cell with Gebhardt. Captain Morris then asked Vaughn if he knew about a party at Willard Sanders when Gebhardt bragged about the murder.

Captain Morris, "And then you know…if you say something in the effect of they asked me about that party. About…"

Vaughn, "Willard's?"

Captain Morris, "Yeah. So apparently, they (the investigators) got some witnesses that heard you say it and they are asking me about it. I can't lie. I can't catch a charge for false statements or something?"

Vaughn, "That would be false statements, a party to a crime of murder. I can't deal with all that. I've already got enough time."

Captain Morris, "So I told him yeah. I didn't lie. And if it…if it…if it takes that to get a (response from Gebhardt)…to get some type of…That's what we need. This is what I think. Because we'll be monitoring it. If there's a response, there of any type of aggression or he's mad or he comes off with I was drunk when I said that…If he gives you any type of indication where he agrees with you that he said that. Or any type of…of uh…BS response like…"

Vaughn, "That some bullshit."

Captain Morris, "(If Gebhardt says) I'm going to kick your ass or something, then what I want you to do is to take your hands and put them behind your head like that and stretch. OK? Because we will be monitoring."

Lt. Harris, "Either that or get out and walk to the door."

Captain Morris, "And we'll come in there and pull (Vaughn) out."

Morris continues, "So you are going to go in. You're going to tell him that you were questioned about if he said that at the party, admitted to killing him (Coggins) at the party and about throwing the knife down the well."

Vaughn, "OK."

Captain Morris, "OK? And when he says what'd you tell them (the officers) or did you tell them anything, even if he don't ask you, you need to let him know I told them I heard that. You know? Just because I heard that don't mean anything. Whatever you need to play it. But you…you need to stress the fact, but you did say it. So, I can't catch a charge for false statements of something how do I know they don't have somebody else recording when I said that and was trying to hem me up. They might have been waiting on me to say no I ain't never heard that so they could play a recording of me hearing it and put me in jail. You know? However, we just…I want you to confront him…"

Vaughn, "With it."

Captain Morris, "Right."
Vaughn, "That way it puts it in his mind."

Captain Morris, "We ain't trying to get him to admit to something he didn't do. All we're trying to do is if you…if we want you go to there and tell him that you were questioned about it, and you admitted it. Because you have been questioned if you…if you…"

Vaughn, "Numerous times."

Captain Morris, "Well and…and…you've been questioned as to whether or not you heard him say he threw the knife down the well and whether or not he killed him at the party, right? That's not a lie. Right."

Vaughn, "Not at the party."

Captain Morris, "Right. You heard (it) at the party."

Vaughn, "That he killed him?"

Captain Morris, "All we want you to do is to go back in there and tell him you were asked those questions and you told us that and that you told us the truth on that and that you had to be honest with us."

Vaughn began to understand what he would be doing when he returned to the cell with Gebhardt. His emotions showed that he was excited about his upcoming time with Frankie. Vaughn even asked if it would be ok to question him about the truck (at the scene of the murder).

Vaughn, "I'll even say something about the truck too and tell him that y'all even heard about the truck."

Captain Morris went over the procedure Vaughn was to follow if Gebhardt became angry or agitated. He assured all that the phone line would be monitored, and Vaughn could pick up the phone for his safety.

Vaughn, "I mean I'm trying the best I can. I wish I had more time. You know what I mean?"

Agent Coleman, "It's alright. You can't force it. It is what it is. It is what it is."

Vaughn was both excited about helping the officers, but also scared to be with Gebhardt again.

Vaughn, "If I can't get him this time. I got parole coming up. Maybe I can make parole. I'll be out there, maybe I can do something. Because he'll be on his turf and he'll feel a little bit better. Right now, you got him already paranoid in there. You know what I mean?"

Vaughn then reminded the officers he was helping them. He asked Agent Coleman for a business card. Coleman did not have one but assured Vaughn that he would get him one.

Vaughn then began to describe his life in prison at Riverbend Correction Facility in Milledgeville, GA. He also promised to help Agent Coleman and the GBI with any investigation they might want to conduct there. "Down at Riverbend. All kinds of crazy shit down there. I'm in there with most of the Mexicans and they (are) actually trying to move drugs on the outside. So maybe we could work something out and do something there too. They already asked me if I knew anybody who sold ice (methamphetamine). So, I don't mind helping y'all any time I can. I get out. I'll…Hell I'll help everybody."

Agent Coleman had made no promises or deals to Vaughn for his cooperation and reminded him, "Good. Well I'm glad you're doing this because it's the right thing."

Captain Morris checked his watch. They had been with Christopher Vaughn for twenty-three minutes. He felt it

was time for Vaughn to go back and question Gebhardt.
Morris reminded Vaughn what he was going to ask. He
reminded him about the party, the knife in the well and if
possible, the truck. Agent Coleman was concerned about
Vaughn drinking the Coca-Cola because he is a diabetic.

Coleman, "Are you ok drinking that Coke?"

Vaughn, "I checked my blood sugar a while ago. It was
about 98."

When Coleman asked Vaughn if they let them have soft
drinks back in the holding areas of the jail, Vaughn said
they did not. But Vaughn didn't want to leave Agent
Coleman without one last plea for an early release
because he was helping.

Vaughn, "I know you can't do a whole lot but maybe you
could at least tell the parole board what I've actually
done. I don't mind doing it."

Captain Morris then led Vaughn back to the cell where
Gebhardt was.

It was to be quite an interesting session.

The Hen Goes back into the Fox den

Vaughn was obviously nervous when he reentered the
cell with Gebhardt. Both his voice and heartbeat could be

heard through the wire. But Vaughn, best he could, tried to control his fears. Though Vaughn himself had committed horrific crimes, he was face to face with Frankie Gebhardt. Gebhardt, or one of his boys, could mess you up real bad if they wanted.

Gebhardt, "Hey."

Vaughn, "They asked me about everything. They asked me about some party at Willard's (Sanders) that you was at. They asked me about some truck."

Gebhardt, remember, is hard of hearing. He kept asking Vaughn to repeat himself.

Vaughn, going through a mental checklist of items the officers had asked him to question Gebhardt about, began to talk louder as he sweated. "A truck."

Vaughn, "Yeah. Supposedly, I guess Bill's truck that was supposedly used that night. They asked me about if the party, if I had ever heard if you had ever said that you killed the boy (Coggins)."

Gebhardt, again squinting his face so he could hear better, "Do what?"

Vaughn, "At...at the party if I ever heard that you killed the boy at Willard's. Uh," Vaughn thought again checking items off his mental list, "They asked about a knife that was supposedly used…that was supposedly used that you threw down the well."

Gebhardt, "Who did what?"

Vaughn, "They asked me about the knife whether it was…if the knife was used…if you threw it down…supposedly down…if you said you ever threw it down your well?"

"Whew," Vaughn thought. All items off the checklist I need to ask.

Gebhardt, "Threw it down my well?"

Vaughn, "They asked me all that."

Gebhardt, "I don't know what they are talking about. Throwed the knife down my well. What f---ing well?"

Vaughn and Gebhardt then discussed which well the knife had been thrown down. There are three wells on Gebhardt's property.

Gebhardt, "I got three wells."

Vaughn, trying to get Gebhardt back on track, "And then they asked me about if I'd ever heard where you was at a party…if I ever head at the party where you admitted that you uh…killed the boy. They asked me about the truck. I told them I don't know about no truck. I was ten years old. I just told them what I know."

Gebhardt replied that, "I don't know what they're talking about. I can't even remember back that far. How'd Bill get that truck. He wasn't even old enough to be driving."

Vaughn and Gebhardt then discussed how old Bill Moore was. At first Gebhardt thought his friend to be about the same age as Vaughn then they agreed that he was closer to Gebhardt's age. Gebhardt agreed that Moore was about, "three of four years older than me." He also related to Vaughn that he, Gebhardt, was born in 1959 or 1960 again depending on who you ask.

Vaughn got back on the subject, "They said they were going to talk to you. They asked me if I ever heard if that you said you killed him (Coggins) or if I ever heard anybody tell me that and I told them what I know. I can't lie to them. Hell, they talking conspiracy to commit murder!"

Gebhardt, "Conspiracy? What's that mean?"

Vaughn, "Wanting to charge me with conspiracy because of not telling what you had done."

Gebhardt, "Well, shit. (Unintelligible)…I'm gonna tell them I can't sign no f---ing paper or nothing. I ain't telling them shit. I can't read."

Vaughn, "You can read, can't you?"

Gebhardt, "Nah hell no I can't read. I ain't signing shit. Not till I get my sister (Sandra Bunn) gets up here. I ain't (unintelligible) them shit."

Vaughn continued to tell Frankie that these were the questions they were asking him. "They damn sure asked me about the knife, whether I had ever heard that."

Gebhardt, "A knife? What about a knife. That's what killed the man (unintelligible) what killed him (unintelligible)….around on me because see they try to turn that shit around. (unintelligible). I ain't telling them shit. I DON'T KNOW NOTHING!"

Gebhardt was beginning to get angry. His voice got louder and louder. Vaughn tried again to reason with him and share what the officers had discussed with him a few minutes ago.

Vaughn, "What do you mean turn it around?"

Gebhardt, "They gonnna say well he told me you said this…he…he…he told me this and all this shit. I'm gonna tell them I don't know a f---ing thing. I'm dumb."

Gebhardt began to smile. He was beginning to understand the drill and why they were trying to use Vaughn. He still didn't know, however, that Vaughn was wired.

Gebhardt, "They can't make me talk to them."

Vaughn, "They got people saying that you said that you killed that boy. They got people saying that you said you killed that boy."

Gebhardt, "I don't care what they got. They got to prove it. They got to prove it. I ain't (unintelligible). I don't know what they are talking about."

Vaughn tried to work the conversation with Gebhardt again. "I said they definitely ask. That's exactly what they got. Because they damn sure asked me. That's one of the first things they were trying to get straight to the point. We got people telling us that Frankie Gebhardt said that he killed that man and he was admitting to it at a party. He was (unintelligible) with him at a party. I don't know if he was drunk or what."

Vaughn and Gebhardt then began to discuss how He (Gebhardt) would get drunk and brag. The party being discussed was at Willard's (Sanders). Vaughn continued to ask Frankie about what he might said in his state of inebriation.

Vaughn, "You ain't never said it (that he-Gebhardt-said he killed Coggins) to anybody when you was drunk?"

Gebhardt, "Not that I know of. When you get drunk, you don't always know what you're doing."

Vaughn, "Son of a bitch. Not that you know of!"

Gebhardt, "I don't know what the f--- I'd say when I got drunk."

Struggling against the sly fox, Vaughn continued to try and get Gebhardt to talk. "Because supposedly there ain't but two of y'all mother---ers that's supposed to know about this shit."

Gebhardt, "Who is that?"

Vaughn said shaking his head, "You and Bill."

Gebhardt, "I don't (know) nothing about it."

Vaughn, "You know they've always said you done that."

Gebhardt, "Yeah."

As the officers came to get Vaughn out of the cell, Gebhardt gave a smile of satisfaction. He had done it again. This "dumb," uneducated man, who could not read or write, who quit school in the sixth grade, had out foxed Vaughn and the lawmen, once again.

Vaughn went into another part of the jail complex to have the wire taken off him. On tape he is heard to tell one of the deputies escorting him, "He just…he..Frankie's got a lot of street smarts. I don't know if you know Frankie. He was in there talking and he said I already know they're going to swap around what you say. I said what do you mean? He said they gonna try to say you said this. I already know they gotta do that. That's the reason I was letting them know when I was…"

Vaughn continued to relay his conversation with the deputy. He shared what Gebhardt has said, or not said, about the party, the murder, the truck and even being drunk.

Harris began to take the wire off Vaughn. "What'd he say…anything?"

Vaughn, "I got him admitting that he can't remember if he ever said it being drunk or not. He said that…I might have did…I can't remember it. I was drunk. Frankie, that's something you need to remember."

Lt. Harris then removed the wire from Vaughn. Several unknown deputies led Vaughn back to his cell. This would be the last taste of freedom Vaughn would enjoy until the trial, which was still over a year away. Vaughn thought about his "detective work with the lawmen," as he left Griffin and returned to Riverbend Correctional Facility in Milledgeville.

In his heart he knew Frankie had won round one. But in his mind, Frankie, the street- smart fox, had really lost. He, Vaughn, was the hero. He had cooperated with law enforcement officials. He knew they would come through and help get him some time off his sentence. Why, he could cooperate in other ways too. He knew if allowed he could work with the lawmen at Riverbend and trap the, "damn," Mexicans selling dope on the outside of the prison walls. Yes sir… he was the hero today. There was no doubt.

Vaughn would return to Riverbend. As he rode the eighty-two miles from Griffin to Milledgeville in the correctional van, Vaughn must have thought to himself that he was a real hero going into the jail cell with his old buddy Frankie Gebhardt, a man he had known since he was 10 years old.

The child molester had to have thought that he was going to get some, "time off," for his bravery going into the cell with the suspect.

Vaughn sits in his small cell at Riverbend every day…hoping…ever hoping…for some sort of consideration for his "deed." After all he had cooperated with the lawmen. He had gotten the brute Frankie Gebhardt to talk. Well almost. There would have to be a reduction in his sentence. It just had to be on the way. In his mind he was a hero. Christopher Joseph Vaughn.

A real hero, for sure.

+++++++

After the trial…

Tuesday, October 9, 2018, thirty-five years after the body of Timothy Wayne Coggins was found off a dirt road near the small hamlet of Sunnyside

Christopher Joseph Vaughn, the self-proclaimed, "hero," still sits in his cell at the Riverbend Correctional Facility awaiting that letter…that word…that telephone call to reduce his sentence.

Thirty-five years to the day, after he, a 10-year old boy, who found the body of Timothy Wayne Coggins in the woods while hunting with his friends…is still waiting.

Eighteen months after he met with Franklin George Gebhardt behind those cold, steel bars, wired to record their conversation…he is still waiting.

Three months after he had testified at the trial, where at one time he had been "the key witness," he…(Christopher Joseph Vaughn)…still waits.

Vaughn is set to be released in October 2054.

October 2054 is a long time away.

Vaughn will be eighty-one years old.

Whatever happened to the 10-year old boy, the whole world, a full life ahead of him?

Whatever happened…no one will ever know. Not even Vaughn can explain what happened to that once innocent young boy.

One fact, however, is known. The child molester, Christopher Joseph Vaughn, the once innocent young man…waits…and waits…and waits…for that word to come.

The phone sits on the warden's desk at the Riverbend Correctional Facility… there is still no word for Christopher Joseph Vaughn.

Chapter 9
"I'm dumb...I can't read."

Thursday, April 27, 2017

Immediately after Vaughn left the cell with Gebhardt, GBI Special Agent Jared Coleman and Spalding County Sheriff Office Captain Mike Morris went into the same area to interview Gebhardt.

The burly bear of a man shuffled through the door in his shackles. He immediately became agitated and defensive with the officers.

"Cause I'm dumb. I can't read," Gebhardt said as he entered.

Agent Coleman, "Just have seat right there for me, Mr. Gebhardt."

Gebhardt, "I don't know what y'all are trying to pull or something else, but I'm fixing to burn some ass up with a lawsuit. Is what I'm fixing to do."

Agent Coleman, "Alright, we are just here to talk to you."

Gebhardt, "I'm fifty-nine years old. I can't read. I can't write. Half-ass dumb. Y'all trying to pull some shit like this on me."

Agent Coleman, "We're just trying to talk to you, sir."

Gebhardt, "No, y'all got me in this mother---er. I would be out taking care of my stuff."

Captain Mike Morris then addressed Gebhardt. "Well Mr. Gebhardt, what you are in here for doesn't have anything to do with it."

Gebhardt, "Yes, it does. That's why I'm in here. I ain't got no subpoena to go to court or nothing. I ain't got none of that. Didn't none of my people get a subpoena or anyone bond me out."

Captain Morris, "Well why do you think…why do you think we are trying to talk to you right now?"

Again, Gebhardt exhibited how hard of hearing he is, "Huh."

Captain Morris, "Why do you think…." Gebhardt abruptly cut him off.

Gebhardt, "I don't know what y'all got up your sleeves. Damn sure don't."

Captain Mike Morris has conducted a thousand interviews with various suspects throughout his career.

He would watch Gebhardt to see if the suspect had certain mannerisms. Eye contact. Posture. The way a suspect does not answer questions gives you signals as to a person's innocence or guilt.

Agent Coleman, "I've got to let you know your rights (Miranda rights) while you are in custody. I can't talk to you while you are in custody without me telling you your rights. OK? I don't have any arrest warrants for you or anything like that. The only reason we are talking here is because this is the time that it came up. If you weren't here, I'd be out there at your house trying to talk to you."

Gebhardt, "It'd be the best place to be talking to me about something, so I'd have somebody with me that's got a little more knowledge than I have."
Agent Coleman, "OK."

Gebhardt, "Because I'm dumb. I mean it. I'm dumb."

Agent Coleman, "OK, well let me read this to you first, and make sure that you understand it and then we'll…"
Coleman was then brusquely cut off by Gebhardt.

Gebhardt, "I don't understand nothing. I'm dumb. I just told you that."

Agent Coleman, "OK. So, you don't want to talk to me?"

Gebhardt, "I'll talk to you all day long."

Agent Coleman, "All right. How far did you go in school?"

Gebhardt, "Sixth grade."

Agent Coleman, "Sixth grade. OK. Can you read and write the English language?"

Gebhardt replied with an emphatic, "NO!"

Agent Coleman, "OK. So, you can't read or write. Can you understand what I'm telling you right now?"

Gebhardt, "I can understand a little bit."

Agent Coleman, "OK. All right. You have the right to remain silent. That means you don't have to talk to me if you don't want to. Do you understand that?"

Gebhardt, "Yes."

Franklin George Gebhardt well knew and understood the requirements as law enforcement officers are required to read the, "Miranda," rights before any interview or arrest is made. After all, Gebhardt had been read these rights dozens of times due to his criminal activity. Stemming from a court case, Miranda vs Arizona in 1966, the law protects individuals from incriminating themselves. After numerous arrests Gebhardt could have recited the law by memory.

Agent Coleman, "OK. Anything you say can be used against you in a court of law. That means that anything you tell me, I can tell a judge. Do you understand that?"

"Yep," Gebhardt smirked.

Agent Coleman continued, "OK. You have the right to talk to a lawyer and have him present with you while you are being questioned. That means if you don't want to talk to me and you want to consult with a lawyer…" Gebhardt cut him off.

Gebhardt, "I can't afford a damn lawyer. I'm a poor man."

++++++++

Note: Once arrested and charged with the murder of Timothy Wayne Coggins in October 2017, Gebhardt and his family did hire a legal team. Larkin Lee and Scott Johnston, who are associated with Virgil L. Brown and Associates, are two of the best defense lawyers in middle Georgia. They represented Gebhardt during the trial and continue to represent Franklin George Gebhardt with his appeals.

++++++++

Agent Coleman, "OK. Well you understand that you have that right?"

Gebhardt, "Yeah."

Agent Coleman finished reading the Miranda Rights law to Gebhardt, "All right. If you cannot afford to hire a lawyer, one will be appointed to represent you before any questioning if you wish. You can decide at any time to exercise these rights and not answer any questions or many any statements. That means that if at any time, you don't want to talk to me, you don't have to talk to me. You understand that?"

Gebhardt, "Yeah."

Agent Coleman, "OK you want to talk to me so you..." he was then cut off by Gebhardt.

Gebhardt, "Yeah. I'll talk all day long now. But I ain't telling you shit I don't know nothing about!"

Agent Coleman, "Why do you think we are here?"

Cunning as ever, the old fox Gebhardt said, "Something about I'm supposed to have killed somebody. Something another is what I heard."

Agent Coleman then asked Gebhardt what he had heard about that and Gebhardt replied, "Umm. Thirty years...about thirty years ago, y'all waxed my ass, if y'all remember. I thought I took a lie detector test and all that shit about thirty years ago."

Agent Coleman, "OK. Well I don't have any information about that in my case file. Tell me what you know about the case."

Gebhardt, "I don't know A DAMN THIING ABOUT IT," Gebhardt replied forcefully.

Captain Morris then asked, "Did you take a...did you take a lie detector test?"

Gebhardt, "Yeah. I took something another back years ago."

Captain Morris, "Who...where did you take it?"

Gebhardt, "Down there at Griffin."

Captain Morris would then try and establish if it was taken at the Griffin Police Department but Gebhardt could not remember. Agent Coleman began to ask Gebhardt a question but was again cut off by Gebhardt.

Gebhardt, "But I don't know why y'all (unintelligible) back in this shit. I ain't never did it. I ain't never thought about doing nothing like that and I won't never do nothing like that. Y'all just as well get off me. I'm out there, nobody but me. My wife (Carole Anne Day Hebeisen Gebhardt) died (July 4, 2012). Fell in my arm(s). COPD. Fell in my arms. I called the (Gebhardt begins to stutter and became unintelligible) …whole side of her head turned purple before I could lay her in the floor."

++++++++

During this point as the audio was played in court a year later, Gebhardt began to cry. Prior to this, the overweight, bald, accused murderer had shown no emotion, no feelings, no reaction. But now, Gebhardt's body began to shake as he sobbed, perhaps thinking about his dead wife Carole Anne, the evidence that had been presented, the audio. It was the first time anyone, the jury, the prosecution, the defense, or law enforcement officers had ever seen Frankie Gebhardt cry. It was as if he wanted to get something off his chest. As if the bully, the thug wanted to admit to the murder. Thirty-four years is a long time to hold something inside. He would never admit he had any part in the murder.

++++++++

Agent Coleman, "I understand, sir. But we are just doing our job. If we get any information, if it was your loved one who had been murdered, wouldn't you want us to follow up on it and try to figure who had done it?"

Gebhardt, "I ain't got to worry about no shit like that."

Agent Coleman, "OK. But if you were in that position, wouldn't you want us to keep looking…." Coleman was again cut off by Gebhardt.

Gebhardt, "Wasn't nobody follow-up on my wife when she fell in my arms."

Captain Morris suggested that maybe the investigators needed to look back into the death of Carole Anne.

Captain Morris then pointed to a cell near Gebhardt. "The guy that's in that cell over there, Chris. What did he say to you?"

Gebhardt, again hard of hearing had to have the question repeated several times. Once he recognized Christopher Vaughn, apparently still unaware of the wire his friend wore and that he had been taped, Gebhardt said, "He didn't say a damn thing to me."

Captain Morris, "He didn't say nothing to you?"

Gebhardt, "No. I've known that boy all my life. Matter of fact, I use to change his diapers. I known him about 45 to 50 years." Vaughn was 45 years old when he went into the jail cell with Gebhardt.

Gebhardt went on to explain how he knew Vaughn's stepfather, Charles Carey, Jr. and how he and Carey built the trailer park that bears his name. "I been in the same place for 59 years. I don't know why y'all keep messing with me. All I got now is a damn ole mule and five dogs," Gebhardt said suddenly turning defensive.

Captain Morris then said, "OK. Look. Listen. What you keep saying y'all keep messing…y'all keep messing with me. I understand that…that you're angry, but me and Agent Coleman have never messed with you before. OK? This is our first time meeting you. OK? So, all we're trying to do do…we're not trying to fuss and bicker and we're not trying to…we've not formed an opinion against you. OK? We're simply here to follow up on some stuff. That's all! We talk about it. It goes to bed."

Gebhardt continued asking why he was in jail and that he wanted to go to court and how he nor anyone in his family had not received a subpoena. "Well something's going on somewhere. Ain't nobody talked to my sister (Sandra Bunn) about it."

Gebhardt would then explain to the officers who his sister was and how her son, Lamar Bunn, worked in law enforcement in Lamar County (Milner). Gebhardt also shared that he was out on bond when he was picked up at his house on a bench warrant. He explained how the home he lived in was actually owned by Lamar, his nephew.

++++++++

Note: At this point, neither Sandra Bunn, Gebhardt's sister, nor Lamar Bunn, Frankie's nephew had been arrested. They would be arrested six months later for, "Obstruction of Justice."

++++++++

Captain Morris, "So Sandy is your sister?"

Gebhardt, "She is the one who takes care of me. After I had a triple bypass and all that, she takes care of me."

Gebhardt went on to explain that he was in a medical cell in the jail because of his heart condition. Once the relationships were established and medical condition explained, Captain Morris then asked, "OK. Well…well listen, this won't take long at all. What we're trying to figure out is so…when…when I'm told they put Chris (Vaughn) in a cell with you over there. And I know I walked over there and saw Chris in your cell. The guy you've known his whole life. He was just in a cell with you I noticed."

Gebhardt, "Yeah."

Captain Morris, "OK. What's up with him?"

Gephardt, "I don't know. All I know is he's been in prison...thirteen, fourteen years. Something like that."

Captain Morris then asked if Vaughn had said anything to or asked Frankie any questions. Gebhardt replied, "Nah."

Captain Morris then suggested that Vaughn's name had come up while they were reinvestigating the murder. "OK. Alright, well uh...Chris name came up."

Gebhardt, "Chris' name came up? I don't know anything about it. I don't know nothing about it. Sure don't!"

Captain Morris then explained the reason they were there talking with Frankie. "Well the reason we are here and what we wanted to talk to you about now is that in 1983 there was a body found. In North Spalding County. A black guy that was found. He was found dead. Off Minter Road."

Gebhardt began to fumble for words, "In '83? How many years has that been? Thirty something years?"

Captain Morris, "It's been awhile."

Gebhardt, "And what y'all messing with me about it for?"

Captain Morris, "Well because...." again cut off by Gebhardt.

Gebhardt appearing to think as he rubbed his forehead. "I wasn't…might have been…wait a minute…fifteen, sixteen at the time. Something like that. Thirty years ago.

Captain Morris, "You are how old?"

Gebhardt, "Fifty-eight." Earlier Gebhardt had stated he was 59. He may have been 60. Who knows for sure?

Captain Morris, "No, you would have been about twenty-seven. And so, we received some information, pertaining to that body, and uh, you know evidence changes and evidence testing changes so Chris' name came up. And so, uh…we recently sent some stuff off to the GBI Crime Lab they found some uh…they analyzed the stuff and found some DNA."

Gebhardt, "After thirty years?"

Captain Morris, "Yes, sir! And uh…there was a…there was a hair sample that was found on the body that was found from somebody that was white. And so. Caucasian, and so…"

Gebhardt looking puzzled, "Whose hair was it? Y'all did the DNA test so you should know."

Captain Morris, "No sir. What I'm trying to explain to you is you have to have something to compare it to, and so what we are doing now is trying to eliminate everybody or positively identify people who were there. And so, we know Chris was up there in the area. We know Chris talked to people, and so what we are trying to do is figure out, how that Chris is older now, so um, we don't know if the hair was found (unintelligible). Was he looking at the body when it was found? That maybe it fell off his head. We just have, we have a hair. OK? And so, we've got to have another hair to compare…." Gebhardt cut Morris off yet again.

Gebhardt, "You want one of mine? You want two of mine? You want three of mine? I don't give a damn. I know I ain't got nothing to do with it."

Gebhardt began to rant and rave about being questioned. He continued to say that he was, "dumb," and, "didn't know nothing about it." He continued to threaten the officers with, "a lawsuit or something." Gebhardt continued to complain, "y'all being on me about something like this? About my pain and suffering and all that? Being in here when I could be out on the street (at home) with my animals."

Captain Morris replied, "I think the real pain and suffering, and who should get the reward for that, is the guy who got killed that day on the powerline. Now Agent Coleman and I haven't been on you on this."

"When you're drunk you're liable to say anything."

Gebhardt would continue to talk for several minutes about feeding his animals. How his name had been, "kicked around," trying to link him to the murder. When asked about being at the party and being drunk, Gebhardt replied, "Now I have drunk for a heap of years now. I was drunk for...I stayed drunk for about 23 years. Now. I'll admit that. I was a drunk for about 23 years. That might be why I'm so f---ing dumb."

Gebhardt would explain to the officers that he forgot and had forgotten many things. "I can tell you I can't remember shit. You can tell me something, and in a minute, I'll have done forgot about it."

Gebhardt, "When you're drunk, you are liable to say anything. Didn't I say that now? I just couldn't drink one beer. I'd just wake up with one in my hand and go to bed with one in my hand. Or have a fifth of liquor in my hand. Or a half a gallon in my hand. Just like I told ya, I'd stay drunk 23 years. I didn't sober up."

Captain Morris, "Do you think that during that time you were drinking that you might have talked about the murder and you just don't remember it?"

Gebhardt, "Nah. I can't say. I ain't going to say because I don't know."

Captain Morris, "What if I told you we had some people who said that they heard you talk about the murder?"

"Tell me who it is, and I'll take care of 'em."

Captain Morris began to show Gebhardt pictures of the deceased. One was Timothy Coggins in the field, body filled with red clay and infested with insects. The other was taken at the morgue. Gebhardt became very defensive.

Gebhardt also wanted to know who was informing the lawmen about and accusing him of the murder.

Gebhardt, "Well, anybody can say what they want to. I can tell you I shit purple would you believe me?"

Captain Morris, "Well I might not believe you when you said it, but if I had four or five other people that said that they say you do it then…" cut off again by Gebhardt.

"Who are the people?" Gebhardt roared. "Who was it. Let's see if I know them. I want to know who them people was."

Gebhardt would ask for a piece of paper and pen to write down the names, even though he said he could neither read nor write!

Captain Morris changed the subject asking where they partied.

Gebhardt, "I'd just go to any folks' houses. Heap of 'em come to my house and party."

Captain Morris, "Who's house? Who's car…who's house would the party be at when Chris (Vaughn) was there?"

Gebhardt, "Might have been his daddy's house. Hell, I don't know. Might have been at his granddaddy's house. I knowed him all my life. I raised up with Bill and (unintelligible) Carey's Mobile Home Park. And Bud Carey brought us plenty of liquor to drink."

Captain Morris continued to question Gebhardt if he remembered talking to anyone about the murder. "That's what we are trying to get to because we are having people telling us that you've talked about it."

Gebhardt, "Tell me some names. Give me some names. Tell me some names. So, I can get in touch with my sister (Sandra Bunn) and tell my sister to talk to them folks and see why they going around and telling shit on me that ain't true. I need to know some names," he demanded. "Will you write me some names down?"

Captain Morris, "Well, I think what we've established is that you are not denying talking about the murder. It's just you're saying if you talked about it, then you might have been drunk, right?"

Gebhardt, "Nah I ain't saying that. NO. DON'T BE PUTTING NOTHING IN MY MOUTH NOW. I SAID I DON'T KNOW. I ain't saying nothing else because I might be...y'all might be trying to twist something around to put this on me."

+++++++

Patrick John Douglas would be another of the, "rogue's gallery," of witnesses the prosecution lined up for the trial. Incarcerated for drugs, meth, violence, firearm violation(s) and other felonies, Douglas was a house manager and trustee in the jail, the same time Gebhardt was incarcerated. He would share that he and Frankie had numerous conversations with each other. Several of the conversations may have centered around the KKK and white power. Douglas, a member of the Aryan Nation Brotherhood, has several (SS) tattoos on his arm, earned for a form of violence against a person of color.

"We were talking about Sheriff Dix one time and Frankie got real irate," Douglas shared.

"Frankie was mad at sheriff (Dix) because a black guy had gotten away (with something) and he asked, 'Why can't I?' Frankie wanted new cell mates so that they could all have different stories," Douglas said. This was an effort by Gebhardt to try and confuse investigators.

"He (Frankie) told me that he was part of the KKK and he was not too worried about the case because there was no DNA and they (the law enforcement investigators) would not find any evidence on the bottle of Jack Daniel's." Gebhardt would then go on to tell his fellow jail mate more than he might should have. "Frankie told me he didn't need any help with that n----- (Coggins). He had thrown him down and stabbed him in the back. (Frankie) told me he just hated n------ in general. He said that he had rescued a white woman from a n----- once before."

Johnathan Bennett is another inmate who heard Gebhardt talking about the murder while in jail. Bennett is serving time for terroristic threats. "I know him (Gebhardt). Him and my mom grew up together. Yes, I heard him bragging about it. He said that he and Mr. Moore (Bill Moore) did it. They were riding in a truck (near Carey's) and said that William Moore stabbed him 38 times," shared later with investigators.

+++++++

Captain Morris assured Gebhardt that he nor any of the other investigators were trying to "twist things around." He then began questioning Gebhardt about the well on his property.

Gebhardt, "Yeah I got a well at my house. Got to drink water, don't I? Matter of fact, I got three wells at my house. The one under my house keeps falling in. Because years ago, years ago my daddy, the corner of the house started falling and my daddy had to redo it."

Captain Morris then asked if he could call Gebhardt by his first name, Frankie. "I don't care," Frankie answered. Conversation began to center once again about what people were saying…about the party…about the knife in the well. Captain Morris could not seem to get Frankie to focus. Gebhardt would continue to go back and forth asking for the names of the people who had accused him.

Captain Morris, "The only other issue we have now is that those same people that are saying that about you also told us that the knife that was used…" Gebhardt interrupts.

Gebhardt, "I need to know who these people is?"

Captain Morris finished his sentence, "was thrown in a well at your house."

Gebhardt, "I need to know who these people is. Well y'all come out there and dig my damn well up. You're welcome too. You can put me in a nice hotel. Come out there and dig my damn well up. Will that solve it?"

Captain Morris, "It would…it would…we may not find a knife but…I need to get down to why you would tell people at parties…" cut off by Gebhardt.

Gebhardt, "I ain't talked to nobody out there I don't reckon. You come out there and dig my damn well up. You're welcome too. Just as long as you make sure I got some more water. I could care less. As long as you furnish me with some water. Cause I don't drink city water."

Captain Morris, "Ok. Alright. We'll see that solves that. You're telling us to come dig the well up and there is no knife there, then we have no reason not to believe you."

The conversation then began to center around the powerline under which Coggins body was found. Again,

Gebhardt was having a hard time hearing the questions. He said he did not remember any murder there. "I don't know nothing about it. That was so damn long ago I don't even know."

"I don't like black folks around me."

Captain Morris asked, "OK. And I understand that. And in 1983 of course things were much different than they are today. So, if you had a uh…young black guy that was up in Sunnyside and he was hanging out with y'all…I mean that was…" Gebhardt cut him off.

Gebhardt, "Well to tell you the truth, I don't hang around with many black folks. Because I don't like black folks around me." Captain Morris suggested that maybe this would jog Frankie's memory. Gebhardt continued, "There ain't been no black folks around me because I don't like them around. The only time I'm around black folks is if I go to the grocery store or y'all put me in here (jail) something like that."

Captain Morris questioned Gebhardt about his work. Gebhardt said that he did some pulp-wooding, worked at the mill and at Florida Rock.

Both investigators were becoming frustrated with Gebhardt's non-answers and, "forgetfulness." Captain Morris asked Gebhardt, "Well I think…I understand that you're being nice. We are having a peaceful conversation and we are just trying to get to the bottom of something, but really you haven't told us a whole lot because what you said is a lot of, 'I can't remember.' "

A heated Gebhardt replied, "I CAN'T! Just like I TOLD YOU before you brought me in here. I'm illiterate. I can't read. I can't write. I can't remember shit."

Agent Coleman quickly picked up the questioning, "What's your relationship with Bill Moore?"

Gebhardt, "He was married to my sister for about 20, 30 something years. Brenda. She died."

Agent Coleman, "Who was your wife around this time?"

Gebhardt, "I didn't have no wife around that time."

Captain Morris, "So you wasn't married in 1983?"

Gebhardt, "No. I didn't get married until I was forty-nine years old."

Captain Morris, "Did you have a girlfriend?"

Gebhardt, "I had a heap of girlfriends."

Agent Coleman then asked Gebhardt, "Who was Micki?" Agent Coleman was looking for an answer if Frankie knew Micki, who also went by the name Ruth Elizabeth Guy.

Gebhardt hemmed and hawed around. "Missy, Missy...Micki...I don't know."

Agent Coleman, "How about Ruth?"

Gebhardt, "I don't know no Ruth. My sister, we call her Sandy Ruth."

Gebhardt would then ask Captain Morris to write the name(s) down for him. Morris refused saying that they were not allowed to give information to prisoners.

Agent Coleman, "Her name was Ruth Elizabeth Guy. Supposedly that was your girlfriend then (1983) and after y'all went to the fair y'all went to her house. You don't remember that?"

Gebhardt, "Nah...uh."

Agent Coleman, "She's dead now."

Gebhardt, "I don't know. I know when all this is said and done I'm gonna see if I can't put a lawsuit on somebody. I gonna do that because my daughter,** she has got a little bit of money. She owns three-fourths of Griffin."

++++++++

Note: Gebhardt's daughter married into a prominent family in Griffin. The author of this book promised a source he would never reveal the name of Gebhardt's daughter. The daughter was named in the transcript from which this chapter is written. Even with the name listed I plan to honor the promise I made.

+++++++

The conversation quickly changed into another completely different direction.

Agent Coleman, "Was there ever an incident where there was a black guy having sex with a girl you were dating?"

Gebhardt, "Nope. Who'd you say that gal was now? When I call my sister, I'm gonna ask." Captain Morris and Agent Coleman would then continue to name Ruth Guy, Micki Guy. Still Gebhardt did not react to the name.

Captain Morris, "You never caught anyone you were dating having sex with a black guy?"

Captain Morris then quickly asked, "You ever killed anybody?"

Gebhardt, "Nah…uh…"

Gebhardt, "Nah…uh…Why you ask me a question like that?"

Captain Morris, "Because we are conducting an investigation a 1983 murder that people are saying you did."

Gebhardt quickly began to say the name, "Micki Guy…Micki Guy…Micki Guy, Micki…"

Captain Morris, "And you don't know anybody that would kill this (young man), laying out there on…" cut off again by Gebhardt.

Gebhardt, "I DON"T KNOW NOTHING ABOUT IT!"

Captain Morris, "I don't think you are being honest with me."

Gebhardt buffed up. Captain Morris thought Gebhardt was going to, "buck," him. Morris got ready for the charge of this caged raging bull. "I can't help what you think," Gebhardt thundered I don't know nothing about it. So, in other words, you are sitting there, calling me a liar."

Captain Morris, "I'm saying that you are not shooting me all the way straight is what I'm saying."
Gebhardt, "You are sitting there calling me a liar."

Captain Morris, "I'm saying that I got a bunch of people…" cut off by Gebhardt.

Gebhardt, "I DON'T CARE WHO YOU GOT."

When Frankie settled back down, Captain Morris began questioning him again about Christopher Vaughn. "How are you with Chris? Are you and him ok?

Gebhardt, "I reckon we are ok."

Captain Morris, "OK. So, you don't think he has a reason to make anything up?"

Gebhardt, "I don't reckon he would. Oh....so you're telling me now he made something up?"

Captain Morris, "No, it would be you saying he made it up."

Gebhardt, "Nah. Well you said he's telling you something. Explain yourself to me!"

Captain Morris would tell Gebhardt that he and Agent Coleman, "had interviewed him a while ago."

Gebhardt, always once again depending on his sister Sandra, "I'm gonna have my sister call his daddy when I get back down yonder (in that) cell."

Captain Morris, "But he's grown. Why would you need to call his daddy?"

Gebhardt, "Because he's been telling that for 13 years. I know. He's been in the chain gang for 13 years."

Captain Morris, "OK. So, would Chris have any…would Chris have any reason…a motive…a reason to make anything up against you?"

Gebhardt, "I don't reckon he would. Folks can do what they want to do. That's just like you can do what you want to do. Just like you sit there and call me a liar. Tell me that I wasn't telling you the truth. Calling me a liar."

Captain Morris, "Well there's things that you can remember. You can remember a lot, and then there is certain things that we need to know, and when I ask you those questions you can't remember. So, you can remember a lot from back then…" cut off my an agitated Gebhardt.

Gebhardt, "No I can't neither. Damn sure can't. You trying to put words in my mouth now and you ain't gonna do it."

Captain Morris, "That's where I need your help in helping me figure out why…if, if, if Agent Coleman just walked into this room right now and told you that I killed somebody, there's either a reason…there's a reason why he would tell you that. Either I killed somebody, or he's got another motive for telling me that."

Gebhardt, throwing his shoulders back, "You know something? He want to walk in there and tell me something like that? I wouldn't care a hill of beans."

Captain Morris, "You wouldn't care if I killed somebody?"

Gebhardt, "Nah..uh. Ain't none of my business. Folks do what they want to do. I don't care. As long as they don't fool with me like y'all fooling with me. Got me in here locked up. Talking my freedom from me for nothing. When the (unintelligible) comes to the bottom, it's gonna come to the bottom. Damn sure will. And when they do, I imagine y'all gonna be looking at me again. Because I'm gonna get my daughter and get a lawyer because I'm fixin' to sue somebody."

The photo…the knife…and Bill Moore

With that Agent Coleman turned the conversation back to Timothy Wayne Coggins. "Did you ever remember seeing this guy?" Coleman showed Gebhardt a photo of victim Coggins again.

Gebhardt, "I ain't never saw him."

Agent Coleman, "There's a pretty good one of his face. Do you recognize him?

Gebhardt, "Nah…uh…never saw him before."

Agent Coleman, "Is there a reason why other folks who were interviewed can identify you as picking him up? There are other people we've talked to who said that they saw you with Bill Moore pick him (Coggins) up."

Gebhardt, "I ain't never met him. I don't know him."

Agent Coleman, "Well there's other people that are saying that."

Gebhardt, "Well I can't say what other people say. I can't help that."

Captain Morris, "Well let me ask you this. A while ago I asked you had you ever told anybody that you killed somebody at a party, and you said you couldn't remember."

Gebhardt, "I don't remember."

Captain Morris, "OK. And I asked you if you ever remembered telling anyone that you threw a knife in the well. And you said you couldn't remember."

Gebhardt, "Nah. I ain't never said that now. That's a damn lie right there now! I ain't never said nothing like that. You trying to twist me around. NO."

Captain Morris, "Well you told us to come dig up the well."

Gebhardt, beginning to fidget and more agitated, "NO. I ain't never told you no shit like that."

Captain Morris, "OK Alright so, you couldn't remember in 1983 whether or not you told somebody you had killed somebody at a party, but you can remember not..." cut off by Gebhardt.

Gebhardt, "That was fifteen minutes ago. I ain't never saw that picture. I ain't never saw that n-----. You trying to say I throwed the knife down the well now. Nah...uh...."

Captain Morris, "I'm talking about the guy in the picture. You never seen him?"

Gebhardt, "I don't reckon I have. I saw a million folks. Do you know everybody you saw?"

Gebhardt was then asked several questions by Agent Coleman and Captain Morris concerning the picture, the knife and the party. Each time Gebhardt said he didn't know, couldn't remember or didn't care what other people said.

Agent Coleman, "But you are not denying it?"

Gebhardt, "Damn right I deny it. I would know if I killed somebody or not. I ain't no damn fool. I might be crazy as hell, but I ain't no fool."

Captain Morris, "Would you tell us if you killed somebody?"

Gebhardt, "You goddamn right I would. I do try to be a half ass man. I do try to be a half ass man. I do try to be straight up and down."

Agent Coleman, "Do you know who killed him (Coggins)?

Gebhardt, "I don't know nothing about it. I done told you that. I don't know nothing about it. I barely can remember them finding him up there."

The questioning then began on whether Gebhardt ever owned or drove a truck.

Gebhardt, "I didn't even have a f---ing (drivers) license for 30 years."

Apparently Gebhardt had a license at one time but lost it due to his arrests. "About 10…about 7…about 8 years ago I got my license."

Gebhardt would tell the investigators that he knew folks who owned trucks and even, "got kin folks that got trucks."

Agent Coleman, "What about Bill Moore? Did he have a truck?"

Gebhardt, "I don't know if he did or not. It's been so damn long."

Captain Morris, "Did Bill Moore drag that guy with truck?"

Gebhardt, "I don't know if he did nor not. Why don't y'all ask him?"

Agent Coleman, "I've already talked to Bill."

Gebhardt seemed surprised by Agent Coleman's answer. Feigning a puzzled look, Gebhardt shot back, "You have?"

Agent Coleman, "Uh huh. That's one of the reasons we are sitting here now."

Quickly changing the subject, Gebhardt asked, "I wish I could see Bill. I haven't seen Bill in 34 years. How's he doing?"

Agent Coleman, "Not too good based on the information he gave me."

Gebhardt, "Huh...the information he gave you? What information he give you?"

Captain Morris, "It's amazing what people will say when they are looking at going to prison!"

Gebhardt, with his anger growing once again, "What information did he give you. I can find out now. I can make a telephone call when I get in yonder. I can find out."

Agent Coleman, "I know you can. Bill know's who killed him (Coggins)?"

Gebhardt, "He does? Well that's his business then."

Agent Coleman, "And based on the information I got from Bill, I think you know who killed him too."

Ever gruff, Gebhardt snarled, "Well that's your business then."

Agent Coleman, "Because I think that you were there then. I think Bill was there."

Gebhardt, Well that's your business then. I can't account for nobody else, but I wasn't there."

Captain Morris, "Do you know if Bill killed him?"

Gebhardt, "I don't know shit. Don't know nothing. But y'all ain't gonna put it on me. You ain't gonna say well tell me Bill told me you did this. Did Bill do that? You ain't gonna turn shit around on me like that. Nuh..uh. I DON'T KNOW NOTHING!"

Agent Coleman, "What I'm trying to figure out is did Bill kill him and you saw it or y'all both hilled him?"

Gebhardt, "Well you dead ass wrong, because I ain't killed nobody. And you dead ass wrong I ain't saw nobody kill nobody. So, you dead ass wrong on both of them."

Agent Coleman, "So why would you say that?"

Gebhardt, "So why are you saying that I killed him? Or Bill killed him?"

Agent Coleman, "Because that's the information that I've got."

Gebhardt, "Well then you've got the wrong damn information. You need to go farther is all I can tell you. Because you ain't putting that shit on me."

Captain Morris, "Who do we need to talk to? Who was all there?"

Gebhardt, "I don't know. I don't even know what you are talking about who all was there. See you trying to say I was there, right there."

Captain Morris, "You said you could find out anything."

Captain Morris then began to ask Gebhardt questions about Broadway Grocery, one of the locations Coggins was allegedly picked up at before he was killed. The other was at the People's Choice nightclub.

Captain Morris, "Do you know where Broadway Grocery is?"

Gebhardt, "Broadway Grocery. Nah…uh…Sure Don't. I ain't never heard of Broadway Grocery. Where's it at?"

Captain Morris, "Down there on East Solomon…East Broadway Street…toward East Griffin."

Gebhardt, "I don't…nah…uh…what about that?"

Captain Morris, "You didn't pick that guy up right there at that store in a truck?"

Gebhardt, "Nah…uh…"

Captain Morris, "Were you in a truck with somebody when they picked him up from the store?"

Gebhardt, "Nah…hu…NO. What else…now what else you gonna bring up? Ask me something else. I need to know about all this shit."

Captain Morris, "I just want to know why. Who did it and why?"

Gebhardt, "There ain't no telling. So, y'all get off my ass. Maybe I can help y'all then. So y'all get off my ass."

Captain Morris, "Why you wanting to help us? A while ago you said you were suing us."

Gebhardt, "I AM !!!! So y'all can get off my ass."

Gebhardt then begins to talk about the pain he has and how his operation nearly killed him. "I got my pain...got me in here suffering. God damn being in this hard cage of lead. Me laying there done had a triple bypass. Don't even want to give me my f---ing medicine."

Captain Morris, "Well I understand you are going through a lot. I understand that uh... that your bed's..." cut off by Gebhardt.

Gebhardt, "Now you are in here trying to tell me that I killed somebody."

Captain Morris, "Well, I'm not trying to tell you that that you did."

Gebhardt, "That's what you said."

Captain Morris, "Can you imagine the pain he (Coggins) was going through while he was being stabbed?"

Gebhardt showing no empathy toward the murdered victim. "That's his problem. You imagine the pain I was going through when I was laying there being operated on? Cut my mother----ing neck to my belly. Laid open. With my heart in your hand."

Captain Morris, "I think he was cut from his neck to his belly too. With a "X" carved into his back."

Gebhardt not hearing a word Captain Morris said. "When they snatch all them needles out of my neck, and all that (unintelligible). You don't think I was in no pain?"

Captain Morris, "Well they didn't cut an "X" in your back and leave you to die though."

Gebhardt, again not paying attention to anyone but himself. "I'd liked to died. That's why they snatched all that shit out of me because it was stopping my nicotine. That's why I quit smoking."

Captain Morris continued, "He (Coggins) didn't a chance to do that. He didn't get that chance. Because he had been stabbed."

Gebhardt, "Well that ain't my problem. I did what I had to do to come back. Well what did you think I was? I was handcuffed down."

Captain Morris, "He (Coggins) was being stabbed violently."

Gebhardt, "I was handcuffed down. Had to break (unintelligible) yank that shit out of me so I could start breathing again."

Captain Morris, "I'm sure while you were being able to breathe again, he (Coggins) was gargling on blood."

Gebhardt finally acknowledged the Captain Morris' points of the conversation. "I can't help him. All I can do is HELP MYSELF! Can't help you. All I can do is HELP MYSELF."

Captain Morris, "We know whoever did it didn't like him (Coggins). They were mad at him."

Gebhardt, "I ain't got nothing. It wasn't me. They mad at him. They shouldn't have made him mad at him I recon' should they?"

Captain Morris, "Whoever, whoever did it to him was mad at him."

Gebhardt would keep saying over and over, "I ain't got nothing to do with it."

Captain Morris continued, "There is a lot of passion involved. They carved an "X" in his back. Pulled his pants down. Drug him around. Pretty violent death."

Gebhardt, "What'd they do that for?"

Captain Morris, "'Cause they were mad at him."

Gebhardt, "Just 'cause they mad at somebody they gonna do all that. I ain't never been that f---ing mad."

Sleeping with Frankie's sister, Brenda

Captain Morris would once again direct the questioning and conversation to Frankie Gebhardt's sister Brenda, Bill Moore's wife.

Captain Morris, "We were told it was you that was mad at him (Coggins) for sleeping with Brenda."

Gebhardt, incredulous, "SLEEPING WITH BRENDA? Brenda was my sister."

Captain Morris, "I know. That's what you were mad about."

Gebhardt, "You a damn lie right there."

Captain Morris, "OK. So, he wasn't sleeping with nobody you knew."

"It became scary, Captain Morris remembered. "He (Gebhardt) was so angry I could tell the mere thought of that, Mr. Gebhardt would become aggressive with us. I actually positioned my body with a table (in case he charged the interviewers). He was angry. ABSOLUTELY."

Gebhardt, looking as if was ready to charge the officers, "But I know my sister better than sleeping with a n-----. I know better than that. Just wait till I call my sister (Sandra Bunn) in a little while. She gonna get your ass, woo-wee."

Gebhardt would then begin hollering, demanding the investigators names and business cards. He kept saying he didn't know (Coggins) and did not recognize his picture.

Captain Morris, "I'm not hollering at you. I don't know why you gotta holler at me?"

Gebhardt, "Cause you keep trying to say I know him (Coggins) and I don't...can't recognize him 'cause I DON'T KNOW HIM."

Captain Morris, "Alright, well, let's take him out of the equation. Is there anybody you knew back then that was sleeping with somebody black you suspected?"

Gebhardt, "NOT MY SISTER!"

Captain Morris, "Okay."

Gebhardt, "But you trying to tell me my sister was sleeping with a n----- That's what you said. And you gonna tell my sister (Sandra Bunn) that too. You gonna tell my sister that when she calls yo' ass cause you damn sure gonna get a telephone call. I promise you that."

Captain Morris answered, "That's fine. I'll answer."

Gebhardt kept asking both Agent Coleman and Captain Morris for their business cards and asked them to write the names of the individuals on it so he could give them to his sister, Sandra Bunn.

Captain Morris, "We're investigating a murder OK. We're going to get to the bottom of it."

Gebhardt, "Somebody's gonna get down to the bottom of it. Damn sure is."

And with that the interview with Gebhardt concluded. It was 12:53 p.m., one hour and six minutes after it had begun.

++++++++

Friday, June 22, 2018, inside the courtroom

On the fifth day of the trial, Assistant District Attorney Marie Broder approached Judge Sams bench and shared, "The Coggins family noticed that Mr. Gebhardt was smiling when in the audio the "N" word was used. It upset them. Maybe Mr. Gebhardt could change places with Mr. Lee (one of the defense attorneys)."

Judge Sams immediately took care of the problem. "I also noticed that Mr. Gebhardt had been looking toward his family members trying to signal them (in some sort of way). Mr. Gebhardt...DO NOT DO THIS AGAIN," Judge Sams warned. Gebhardt, Lee and Johnston all nodded their heads in agreement and understanding with Judge Sams' directives. Gebhardt then looked back at his sisters Sandra and Pauline and smiled.

++++++++

Agent Coleman and Captain Morris both wondered as they left the jail and their interview with Franklin George Gebhardt. It had been a, "full and taxing day," for the investigators.

How were they going to get to, "the bottom of it?"

The bottom of Frankie Gebhardt's well!

Chapter 10
Arrests are made, and the winds
of change begin to blow

1993-2014 Frankie and Bill

Not ashamed of what he had done, a cagier Gebhardt would get drunk, and tell anyone who would listen, "I miss the good old days when you could kill a n----- for no good reason." His bragging and threats continued. Ten years down the road, in 1993, another witness saw Gebhardt threaten his girlfriend at the time, pushing, knocking and shaking her around. "I told you woman. Quit your bitching and shit. If you keep on, you're going to end up like that n----- in the ditch."

Life continued pretty much the same. Drinking, f---ing, a little work here and there and lots of arrests and jail time. Gebhardt and Moore would accumulate over seventy arrests and time in jail between them. (See rap sheets for both Gebhardt and Moore at end of the book).

On August 11, 2006, Frankie would marry Carole Anne Day Hebeisen in the front yard of the family home. He seemed to have settled down with his wife. They had no children. Carole Anne even got Frankie to go to the Sunnyside Holiness Church, but he soon quit because he felt people, "were looking down on him." They lived a simple life. Frankie cut up his own meat., had chickens on his property. Frankie's nephew, Lamar Bunn, described the couple. "They weren't nothing to look at, didn't have a pot to piss in, but they loved each other. They seemed to be real happy."

But the happiness would not last. Frankie and Carole Ann began to fight. And as with many of his girlfriends, Gebhardt began beat his wife. This time, however, Carole Ann stood her ground. Once when Frankie pushed his wife to the ground, Carole Ann got up and threw a brick at Frankie hitting him between the eyes and knocking him out.

Suddenly, the happiness and fighting would end. After a short six years of married "bliss," Carole Anne Day Hebeisen Gebhardt died at their home, July 4, 2012. The story was that Frankie tried to revive his wife with CPR but failed. Ruled a natural death, authorities still wonder if the death was indeed, "natural."

Bill Moore's wife, Frankie's baby sister Brenda, would die two years later, April 26, 2014. Bill never really got over her death. Even though divorced at the time, they would work together to raise their son and daughter. "She was everything to me," Moore related to the author in an interview with tears in his eyes. "To this day, I really miss her."

The "Dons of Sunnyside," continued their boasting and bragging. They were feared by all because Franklin George Gebhardt and William Franklin Moore were "the real deal." Gebhardt had killed once. He bragged about it. Fear was he would kill again, perhaps he had. No one really knew. But those who lived in and around Sunnyside were tired of the threats, the anger, the evil ways these two continued to exhibit. Good, honest, hard-working citizens of the area were weary of living in the dark. It would soon be a new day. The rampaging days of murder and mayhem were almost over. Justice could be seen on the horizon. Gebhardt's and Moore's days of freedom were numbered.

In April 2017, Gebhardt was once again locked up for *False Imprisonment, Battery and Sex Crimes*. It was all about to come down upon Frankie. This time he would not get out of jail so easily.

Behind bars….locked up.

People felt now, now they could talk. And talk they did.

A new sheriff was coming to town.

November 2016

Darrell Dix was elected Spalding County Sheriff in November 2016. He would begin his four- year term in

January 2017. The election for sheriff had been a hotly contested primary, followed by an even more brutal general election. Dix won both. Even though most everyone in the Spalding County community knew and genuinely liked and admired the homegrown man and his family, he had to spend a lot of time and money on the campaign trail. It was a, "Hometown Boy Makes Good," type story.

The newly elected sheriff served in the Griffin Police Department almost three decades. Dix knew his community and had been a part of the good…and ugly. He had worked both in the public information side of law enforcement to the narcotics side. Dix helped save numerous lives and worked with the Special Olympics of the community. The new sheriff knew the highs and lows of law enforcement having been named officer of the year and "Best of the Best," then watching others die before his eyes.

Darrell Dix loved his hometown community. And his hometown loved him.

It was not unusual then that the new sheriff was about to shake things up.

The cold case was about to heat up…again.

But this time there was hope. A new hope suspects would be found and tried for the brutal slaying of Timothy Wayne Coggins.

In 1983, when Coggins was murdered, there were 19,310 murders in the United States. Averages show that about 43 murders a day occur in the United States. Many of the cases are solved immediately. Many are deemed "cold cases," or unsolved cases. Within the US approximately 30% of the murder cases go unsolved each year. That means the chances of a murder case being solved is only about 60-70% to begin with. If a case continues to be, "cold or unsolved," the rate for cracking the case goes down dramatically each year as the case(s) lies dormant.

Of the "cold cases," in America only 5% of the suspects are arrested. Of those arrested only 1% end in convictions. Chances are so small that only 1 in 1,300 cases are ever solved, most with the use of Deoxyribonucleic Acid tests, or DNA. Simply put this is the genetic code each person has within their body. DNA testing did not come about until 1990. Even then many states hesitated to use it to solve a case. But as the testing became more efficient and positive, DNA swipes were used to solve murder cases. The case of murder against Timothy Wayne Coggins occurred in 1983, seven years before the introduction of DNA in crime scenes. In

2017 the case had been, "cold," for 34 years. One would think, "unsolvable." Percentages were against the Coggins family ever finding an answer of who actually murdered their loved one.

January 2017

After the election, Sheriff Dix began to reexamine the Coggins case. He made solving this case a…TOP priority.

Dix thought back. So much has changed since 1983, when he entered Griffin High School. Witnesses began to recall that night long ago when Coggins was killed. They shared with Sheriff Dix what they knew about Gebhardt and Moore's possible involvement. "It would not be an easy case to solve or revisit," Dix thought. "But it's important to our community and the Coggins family. They need some justice and peace. It's a long shot we just gotta take."

Friday, October 13, 2017

Calls had come in from all over the United States about the 34-year old, "cold-murder case." Sheriff Dix answered each call giving them his personal attention. He didn't want to let on to how much he knew because Dix knew facts, evidence and corroborating witnesses would be hard to round up if known. He'd best keep silent. Sheriff Dix had learned from several witnesses they had known about the death of Coggins but, "had been afraid to come forward," due to the fear of retribution from Gebhardt or his comrades.

Frankie Gebhardt knew something was up. The old Sunnyside gang had suddenly quit answering his phone calls from prison. They had turned their back on him. Visitors were now few and far between for the burly, foul mouthed, bear who liked to threaten and give orders forever expecting these orders to be carried out by others. No questions asked. Better to claim he knew, "nothing about it," as he had told Captain Mike Morris and Special Agent Jared Coleman only a few months before.

So, it came as no surprise, Friday, October 13, 2017, five people were arrested in connection of the murder of Timothy Wayne Coggins. Frankie Gebhardt being one of the five. The arrests came exactly 34 years and four days to the date the 23-year-old African American man's body was found murdered in the woods of northern Spalding County.

If you believe in astrological signs, Frankie Gebhardt, a Leo, was warned in his horoscope, that day, "Watch out.

Boastful ways and angry spirits will bring you down this day (Friday, October 13, 2017)."

Franklin George Gebhardt and William Franklin Moore, Sr., were arrested and charged with five counts:

1) Murder

2) Felony murder

3) Aggravated assault

4) Aggravated battery

5) Concealing the death of another

Three others, Sandra Bunn, who is Frankie's sister; Lamar Bunn, who is Frankie's nephew and Gregory Huffman, who worked in the Spalding County jail, were charged with "Obstruction of Justice." Huffman, as a duly sworn state officer, was also charged with violation of oath of office. Lamar Bunn, who at the time of his arrest, was a Milner, GA policeman, was fired soon thereafter.

Sheriff Dix and his deputies rounded up the group and took them to the Spalding County Detention Center for booking and processing. Dix would contact the original investigators in the case, Oscar Jordan and Clint Phillips. "I wanted them to be there when the handcuffs were put on," Dix said. Phillips, who himself could not be present at the arrest, had just had open heart surgery. But Jordan, who had suspected the duo of the horrible crime years ago, could not have been more pleased. Two pairs of handcuffs were placed on Gebhardt and Moore. Gebhardt was led back into the Detention Center by Sheriff Darrell Dix on his left, who was wearing his trademark Stetson and Investigator Oscar Jordan, wearing a dark suit and tie on Gebhardt's right. Gebhardt was wearing his prison uniform (as he was still in prison for the earlier charges of sexual battery) and orange flip-flops. His bald head and with his gray goatee downcast. Buttons on his striped prison suit were almost bursting open from the weight he had gained. Gebhardt looked much older than his 59 (or 60) years.

Jordan walked into the front door with tears in his eyes. It was a day he knew was long in coming. Jordan was presented one of the pair of handcuffs Gebhardt wore into the center. Sheriff Dix smiled, shook Jordan's hand and said, "You've waited 34 years for this. You've earned them." Sheriff Dix would also make sure Phillips received a pair of the handcuffs.

Bill Moore, on the day of his arrest, wore a bright red shirt, white shorts and dark tennis shoes. He had been arrested at his home. Moore was haggard looking and dejected as he was led into the detention center. Captain Mike Morris was on Moore's left and GBI Special Agent Jared Coleman on his right as they led him through the steel prison doors. Other deputies and GBI investigators were also on the scene. Moore looked down and didn't really seemed surprised with the arrest. "The Sunnyside Pussy," a nickname Moore had earned because he carried a baseball bat around with him at all times, had heard talk around town and thought something might be, "coming down."

The story of the arrests made front page news not only in the local newspaper, *The Griffin Daily News*, but also in the state newspaper, *The Atlanta Journal Constitution*. Television reports on CNN and Fox News showed the five accused handcuffed with mug shots glaring back at the reader and viewer. It was big news. After 34 years to have suspects arrested in a cold murder case was news…BIG news.

Bond Hearings

Sandra Bunn, Lamar Bunn and Huffman were arrested at their homes as well. They too were led into the detention center, mug shots taken, fingerprints made. When arrested in Georgia, certain charges allow one to post bond. Murder is not one of them.

Sandra Bunn (the same sister Frankie said was going to, "sue everybody"), Lamar Bunn (Gebhardt's nephew and Sandra's son), had been charged with "Obstruction of

Justice." They were released on a $10,000 bond each the same day as their arrest, Friday, October 13, 2017. Each paid $706.75 for their bond(s). Huffman, who worked with Spalding County at the time as a jailer in the Spalding County Detention Facility, was released Saturday, when he posted a $10,000 bond for the obstruction charge and $20,000 for the violation of office he had been charged with.

Gebhardt and Moore faced Magistrate Don Taliaferro early Saturday morning to learn of their fate. Judge Taliaferro denied bond from the courtroom within the Spalding County Detention Center for both Gebhardt and Moore, due to the five charges, two of them for murder. Both would return to their nearby cells after the hearing.

Sheriff Dix realized there was a lot of work ahead of him. He praised the media for helping with the case. "Media coverage generated new leads that were key to solving this case." But Dix also knew incalculable man hours, hard detective work, and lots of, "plain good old investigation," had brought about the downfall of Gebhardt and Moore.

The sound of the clink of the steel handcuffs on both Moore and Gebhardt was sweet. But Sheriff Dix knew they had to get into that dry water well to find tangible evidence for the trial. Testimony from convicts and ex-cons would not sway a jury.

How…how were they going to get into that well on Gebhardt's property?

Gebhardt had been using the telephone in the jail facility to make personal calls. Inmates are allowed use of the telephone. Even after his interrogation with Captain Morris and Special Agent Coleman, Gebhardt thought he was invincible. In several of the calls Gebhardt made from prison he told the person*** on the other line he knew exactly what was going on and what the investigation was all about. Frankie did not realize or maybe forgot that telephone calls from inside the prison are recorded. There is a sign posted. But then again, Frankie could not, "read or write.

Other prisoners were too afraid to tell him! Gebhardt's ace in the hole was the fact was he knew the lawmen would not be able to dig out the well near his house. It would destroy the integrity of the foundation of the home. If they dug and found nothing, Spalding County owed him a new house. As Gebhardt hung up the phone, he smiled and thought he could use his get out of jail free card yet again. Little did he realize that many of the residents of Sunnyside and Spalding County Frankie had intimidated, were now talking to the sheriff and GBI. Gebhardt thought that a number of people on the outside, "had it coming and I'm gonna whup some ass. Uh huh," when he "got out."

But Spalding County had the bigger stick this time. Gebhardt was going to court for the murder of Timothy Wayne Coggins. Spalding County District Attorney Ben Coker and his staff didn't know how they would win a guilty verdict from a jury. Their case was shaky at best. The prosecution's key witness was a convicted child molester. But Coker and his team knew one thing for sure. They would have to, "find the answer," hopefully at the bottom of that well.

Sometime in the spring, 2018

Coker, as well as Sheriff Dix, knew they had to get into that well. A graduate of Griffin High School, the University of Georgia and Georgia State Law School, Coker became Spalding County District Attorney when elected in November 2016. He replaced Scott Ballard, who had run for Superior Court Judge of the Flint River Judicial Circuit and won. Coker knew this was one of the biggest cases of his young career. But how would he get inside that well?

The investigative team, GBI agents, Sheriff deputies and district attorney staff were in the meeting room, just outside the DA's offices. The initial thinking was that they would get a well drilling company to come onto the property, drill down the typical way and then examine cores of dirt brought to the surface. Perhaps GBI scientists could analyze the samples and determine dates of the soil and any burning residue that might be found. This was a long shot at best. Coker and his team knew it.

Then suddenly Captain Mike Morris remembered he had heard of a new type of drilling that used water pressure and a vacuum to suck out the contents of a well or marshy area. The name of the company was Atlanta HydroVac located in Woodstock, GA. Maybe they could use the hydrovac system to excavate and suck out what was in that well. It might just be worth a try.

"Let's give 'em a call," Coker said. "This might be our one shot."

Hydrovac uses a method akin to that of a shop vac. The company goes into a hole, pond, marshy area, and literally sucks the contents out into a large tanker truck. The truck is driven to wherever needed and contents discharged. "This might just be the answer," Captain Mike Morris thought. "This might just work."

Frankie Gebhardt could hardly be contained. He would roar out loud and rattle the steel bars of his small jail cell when he thought about being arrested for the crime of this "n-----." Fellow inmates would tread lightly around Gebhardt. They knew he was volatile and could fly off the handle at any time, for no apparent reason. The monster had been caged, for now.

Don't be fooled by her good looks
or syrupy southern drawl

Once Gebhardt and Moore had been arrested Assistant District Attorney Marie Broder was assigned the case by Coker. It was a perfect choice. Broder is a beautiful southern lady. Petite and slim, Broder is not what you would picture as a prosecuting attorney. Broder's sweet, southern molasses drawl draws a smile when you listen to her speak. But don't let that fool you. In the courtroom, she is all business. Broder wants the win and conviction for the State of Georgia every time. "I want to find the truth in every case," she smiles. "I don't like to be lied to, by either side," her smile turning into a cold stare. "Beyond all question, I want the truth."

The truth is, when the defense goes into the courtroom to try a case, Broder is already ahead by a touchdown before the trial even begins. Broder and her team come prepared...well prepared, to show the jury the truth of the case. At the end of the day Broder says that it is 12 people from Spalding County that will decide if the truth has been told or not. "That jury is searching for the truth. I never promise a family I will find someone guilty...only that the truth will be found. Families deserve to have peace. To get 12 folks (the jury) to find that truth...WOW."

Her full name is Marie Elizabeth Greene Broder. She grew up in nearby Thomaston. Her family owns a successful propane business. But it was not a sheltered life growing up for Broder. "We traveled a lot. My mother and father, Elizabeth Peggy Greene and Mike Greene wanted me and my, 'Irish Twin,' brother Tony, to learn about the world. They wanted us to realize there is more to this world than just Thomaston, GA," she said.

Marie's mother taught special education and gave Marie the core to her spirit that, "it was possible to change the world." Broder attended the local Thomaston schools later leaving for Athens and the University of Georgia. Starting out wanting to be an investigative reporter Marie graduated with a double major, journalism and speech communication. But perhaps the one thing that steered her toward law was a meeting she held her junior year at

UGA with her mother's father, her grandfather, Arlis
Burch. Burch who lived in Douglas, GA, "was the
American Dream. He grew up with 14 brothers and
sisters, went into the military, studied hard and became a
dentist."

During her life Broder had always heard a story about
how one of Arlis' brothers was killed. But didn't know the
circumstances of the murder.

"When I told my grandfather (Arlis) I had decided to
become a lawyer, he got real emotional and teared up.
Arlis' brother was at Auburn when he was stabbed and
killed. The murderer received a minimum seven-year
sentence and would only serve three and a half years of
that sentence. This really destroyed my mother. He
(Arlis) and I both knew then that being a lawyer…a
prosecutor…was something where I could really make a
difference."

Right then and there, Marie Greene (Broder) decided to
become a prosecuting attorney. She has never looked
back.

Out of the 35 murder cases Broder has tried (toward end
of 2018-including Gebhardt and Moore), 16 received life
sentences (14 found guilty by a jury and 2 pled guilty).
One particular-case she remembers, was when the killer

of an off-duty policeman, Kevin Jordan, was given a life sentence.

Another was the conviction of Steven Spires, a child molestation case. It is said that her closing arguments during the case were some of the finest ever heard in the Spalding County courtroom. It took the jury only an hour to find Spires guilty. Broder who is married to a local attorney, Karl, with whom they have a four-year-old daughter, said that when Spires daughter was on the witness stand, "it was very tough. Very hard. I too have a daughter. I am a mother. Ben (Coker) is a great boss. He gave me some sage advice during that trial. Remember you are also a prosecutor. I will never forget that...ever."

Broder, who does not watch television law and order type shows because "she wants to forget about that part of her life for a bit," does enjoy time with her family and reading romance novels. Maybe it is in the romance novels she finds the battle between good and evil. "I will continue to do what I can because it really is all about good and evil. I want to continue to fight for the good. This job is hard, so tough. But it is so very rewarding."

Franklin George Gebhardt had met his match. This petite southern brunette beauty would be the person who would stand up for justice and finally take on Gebhardt, the Sunnyside thug, even after 34 years.

Wednesday, November 1, 2017

Gebhardt's and Moore's attorneys began to scramble to try and get their clients out of jail. On Wednesday, November 1, 2017, the attorneys appeared in Judge W. Fletcher Sams courtroom pleading for bond. Spalding County District Attorney Ben Coker argued that both Gebhardt and Moore, "posed a significant threat to the community." Coker continued, "Witness intimidation in this case has been systematic for 34 years." But Coker relayed to Judge Sams that, "new and original witnesses have come forward saying that they had been threatened by the defendant(s) and were too scared to reveal their knowledge."

David Studdard, Frankie Gebhardt's original attorney approached the bench and shared with Judge Sams, "My client has no idea about any of this. He doesn't know anything about this." Studdard continued, "(Frankie) is not a flight risk. He has lived in Spalding County for over 50 years and (that) he is poor health as well." Referring to the original reason Gebhardt was in jail, sexual battery, Studdard asked Judge Sams, "We don't expect the court to treat this case lightly, but Mr. Gebhardt would like to have the opportunity to at least make bond at the end of his misdemeanor sentence."

Kevin Hurt, Moore's original attorney, pled with the court pointing out, "my client is not fit to flee or to intimidate witnesses. He is disabled from back surgery."

Judge Sams considered the pleas for only seconds before denying bond. "Because of the defendants' long criminal history and intimidation of witnesses, bond would be inappropriate. Bond(s) denied."

Thursday, November 30, 2017, Probable cause hearing

Both men appeared before Spalding County Magistrate Judge Rita Cavanaugh on Thursday, November 30, 2017, a cool, foggy November morning. Judge Cavanaugh is not a judge to be trifled with. One would never suspect the gentile; ever charming southern lady is as tough as any judge in Spalding County. She has seen it all from her bench in the Spalding County jail complex. This was one of the few times an overflow audience packed the room. Both Gebhardt and Moore had new attorneys at the hearing. Gebhardt had hired criminal legal defense firm Virgil L. Brown and Associates of Zebulon with Larkin Lee and Scott Johnston making up his defense team. Moore, on the other hand, pled a lack of funds to support a private attorney. Harry Charles, Georgia Public Defender represented Moore.

Ben Coker and Marie Broder represented the district attorney's office and sat at their table.

Lee, Johnston and Charles, along with Moore and Gebhardt, sat at the table for the defense.

Family members of Coggins, Moore and Gebhardt sat in silence in the jailhouse courtroom as the hearing began.

Cordial and charming as ever, Judge Cavanaugh greeted the early morning audience and asked the deputies to bring the suspects into the courtroom. When the suspects entered, it would be all business. Judge Cavanaugh knows the law.

Frankie Gebhardt came in first surrounded by Spalding County Sheriff Deputies. His eyes, black as coal, stared straight ahead. He never looked toward his or Coggins family members. Bill Moore was wheeled in next in a wheelchair. Moore seemed repentant with his eyes cast downward. Gebhardt arrogant and brutish as always in his appearance.

Judge Cavanaugh began the proceedings with a summary of the charges against the two men. The prosecution and defense both had opening summaries of the case.

A key witness, Jared Coleman, Special Agent with the Georgia Bureau of Investigation, was asked to take the stand to relay his findings of the investigation. Coleman began by stating the investigators had determined that the murder was racially motivated. Multiple witnesses had told Coleman and law enforcement they had heard the suspects discuss the murder several weeks and even years afterwards. Coggins crime, "dancing with a white woman."

Coleman shared with Judge Cavanaugh that based on evidence he and others had collected, Gebhardt and Moore believed, "they were doing the right thing," by killing Coggins and that they were, "protecting the white race from black people." Moore had even told witnesses and those gathered at a party at Carey's that he, "missed the good old days when you could kill a n----- for no reason." There was a slight gasp from the audience and reporters present after this statement was made. Moore, perhaps drunk, or better yet wanting to fit in with the unruly crowd, had even bragged to several of his friends' weeks before they were arrested that he, "was the one to stab (Coggins)."

GBI Special Agent Coleman continued his testimony telling how both Gebhardt and Moore, who carried a baseball bat with him, had intimidated witnesses and people they knew telling them not to testify against them. Coleman also brought out that a drug deal, "gone bad," may have been another reason for the murder as well as a relationship between Coggins and, "Gebhardt's old lady."

Agent Coleman had been assigned the cold murder case in 2015. He testified that since his assignment several witnesses had come forward with new information.

When Coleman's testimony concluded, Judge Cavanaugh ruled there was enough evidence to bind the case over to a Spalding County Grand Jury, which was scheduled to meet again early the next week, December 5, 2017. The hearing had taken a little over an hour.

Gebhardt and Moore's attorney both had things to say about the case when Judge Cavanaugh dismissed the courtroom. Larkin Lee, Gebhardt's attorney shared that this was one of the toughest cases he had ever handled. "You know as much as I do at this point. We're going to have to piece it together, and it's going to be difficult to (piece together) 1983 again."

Harry Charles, Moore's attorney, stated, "Mr. Coker knows (he cannot win this case). His witnesses are the scum," referring to Vaughn and others who were in jail themselves.

Gebhardt was escorted out, Moore wheeled out, both to their nearby cells to await the Grand Jury's findings. For now, both would remain incarcerated.

Tuesday, December 5, 2017, Grand Jury meets

On Tuesday, December 5, 2017, the September Term 2017 Spalding County Grand Jury met at the courthouse. The nine female and ten male members found that Gebhardt and Moore should (true bill) stand trial for the murder of Timothy Wayne Coggins and would be bound over to the Spalding County Superior Court.

The duo was charged with five counts:
1) Malice Murder (O.C.G.A. 16-5-1 (a))
2) Felony Murder (O.C.G.A. 16-5-1 (c))
3) Aggravated Assault (O.C.G.A. 16-5-21)
4) Aggravated Battery (O.C.G.A. 16-5-24)
5) Concealing Death of Another (O.C.G.A. 16-10-31)

Originally the case was number 17R-524 A&B but would be changed due to a technicality in the wording.

Gebhardt and Moore were scheduled to appear in court on January 25, 2018, to be arraigned.

Now it was the defense attorneys turn to get busy.

End of 2017 into 2018, Motions and more motions

Defense attorneys Lee, Johnston and Charles had their work cut out for them. Motion, upon motion upon motion would begin to be filed by the Gebhardt legal team. Moore sat waiting, waiting and waiting. It didn't seem as if his attorney Harry Charles was interested in defending his client. No motions were filed on behalf of Moore by the public defender during the pre-trial hearings.

- On December 28, 2017, Larkin Lee wasted no time in filing a motion that the case be dismissed due to the statute of limitations. He plead that after 34 years there was no way that everyone could remember the details of the murder or the evidence found in the case. *Motion was later denied.*

- On January 16, 2018, a witness list comprised of 92 names was submitted to the court and to the defense by the district attorney (the list would end up at 103 names). An additional three names would be added to the list in the spring. Of the witnesses half-a dozen were either in jail or had been in jail for felony offenses. The prosecution's case was still shaky due to the fact they had not yet found the means to drill the well next to Gebhardt's property.

- The defense asked that Frankie Gebhardt be given a mental evaluation to see if he was able to stand trial. The consent order was granted by Judge Sams on January 16, 2018. Gebhardt would be evaluated by state mental health experts and the report shared with the judge, the defense and the prosecution.

  (Note-this was the second time Gebhardt had taken a mental evaluation to see if he was fit to stand trial. The other given years before for another crime. Interestingly enough, his attorney at the time of his first mental evaluation, was Harry Charles, the same attorney that now represented Frankie's brother-in-law, Bill Moore).

- January 16, 2018, Larkin Lee, Gebhardt's attorney, asked that special consideration be taken in the charges against his client could be confusing. A "Special Demurrer," was filed showing that such cases had confused jurors and due to the, "special defects," in the language of the charges the charges be thrown out. *Motion was later denied.*

- Thursday, January 25, 2018, both Gebhardt and Moore were arraigned in court. They appeared before Judge W. Fletcher Sams and pled not guilty. It was pointed out that Gebhardt had a pending mental evaluation and that March 19, 2018, had been set aside as a date motions from both the prosecution and defense would be heard and considered.

- In a bombshell, but not an unexpected move, Defense Attorney Larkin Lee filed a motion that a change of venue should be given to his client Gebhardt. Lee claimed in the petition and motion that Gebhardt had received unfair publicity by not only the local, but statewide newspapers and media and that a fair trial would not be possible in Spalding County. Lee requested that the trial be moved out of Spalding County. *The motion was later denied.*

- On January 30, 2018, the state and Judge Sams issued a "Scheduling Order" for the motions, hearings and trial to take place. A motion hearing to consider the motions from both prosecution and defense was scheduled for March 16, 2018. A "Voir Dire," which Judge Sams issued so that potential jurors could be asked questions to determine if the trial venue was needed was set for April 27, 2018. (*This would not take place as Judge Sams ordered that prior publicity had not affected any potential jurors. Questions, however, were asked during the jury selection if they had been prejudiced by the media coverage of the case*). A trial date of June 18, 2018 was established in the "Scheduling Order" approved by Judge Sams.

- February 8, 2018, the defense team asked that the court make sure they received all the evidence the prosecution had gathered be given to them. This included rights to inspect, photocopy, and have available other tangible evidence so they could build their case. *The motion was later approved.*

While the motions and file of motions for Gebhardt grew in the Clerk of Superior Court's office, Moore continued to wait. Upon inspection, Moore's file was as small as ever. A man with little to no money, Moore could not hire the legal defense team Gebhardt's relatives had gotten. He was literally at the mercy of the state with an attorney who filed no motions on his behalf.

- Larkin Lee and Scott Johnston complained that they had not have private access to their client, Frankie Gebhardt, while he was incarcerated. They complained they had to meet with their client in holding cells, in hallways and even speak over a phone where there was a warning that all, "communications are recorded." The team complained that this was in violation of client attorney privilege. *The motion was later approved.*

- In another surprise, but again not unexpected move, the Gebhardt defense team filed a motion to, "Sever the Trial of the Defendant (Franklin George Gebhardt)." A four- page petition and motion was filed in the court on February 8, 2017. Gebhardt would now leave his, "friend, his brother-in-law behind," *as the judge agreed to the motion.* Gebhardt and Moore would now have separate trials. There was speculation later that the motion to sever and have separate trails was because Gebhardt's defense team did not want Moore to testify against their client. One will never know!

- The Gebhardt defense team asked the district attorney to inform them of any deal, consideration, promises or grants of immunity that was issued prior to the trial. This was mainly pointed toward

Christopher Joseph Vaughn who was a key witness for the prosecution and was sentenced to jail for 50 years for child molestation. *This motion was later approved.*

- The motion hearing scheduled for March 16, 2018 was delayed. This was due to the fact the mental evaluation on Franklin George Gebhardt had not come back. Judge Sams and the attorneys for both sides would retire to the judge's chambers and make a call to the state evaluators asking them when to expect the report.

- The March 2018 Term of the Spalding County Grand Jury met, March 19, 2018, to clear up some of the legal language from the early indictment. The twelve female and eight male members of the jury approved the changes. The cases would now be tracked by their respective numbers through the court system: Gebhardt 18-R-105A and Moore 18-R-105B

- The hearing earlier scheduled for March 16, was held on March 22, 2018. Judge Sams and attorneys from both sides met in judge's chambers to discuss the mental evaluation of Frankie Gebhardt. When the group returned to the courtroom, Judge Sams reported, "I feel it is safe to proceed with the motions hearing." Gebhardt had been evaluated as, "fit to stand trial." Judge Sams also ruled at the hearing:

-Both sides instruct witnesses not to testify in hearsay

-Law enforcement and agencies must save any and all notes related to the case and make available to the defense

-Gebhardt and Moore will have separate (sever) trials

-A motion to change venue of the trial was still under consideration

-Another motion hearing would be held April 20, 2018

Thursday, April 12, 2018, Winds of change begin to blow

The morning came and as usual Gebhardt was awakened in his cell. Confident as ever with his new defense attorneys, Frankie ate his usual breakfast. As the eggs went down his throat, things were about to change and rock Franklin George Gebhardt's world.

This was the day the team from Atlanta HydroVac left Woodstock even earlier than Frankie had gotten up. The team headed south down I-75 toward Griffin. The GPS on owner Greg Dubin's phone showed the truck exactly where to pull off. It was down US Highway 19/41, just past a little hamlet named Sunnyside, onward toward 1704 Patterson Road.

They had a job to do today.

It was the first-time any State of Georgia investigator would use a hydrovac system to collect evidence used in a trial.

The winds of change were blowing.

Things were about to go south for Gebhardt. He just didn't realize how bad things were going to get when he woke up that morning.

Chapter 11
A shoe at the bottom of the well

Dry water well set to be drilled

The old, now dry, water well, the one next to Frankie Gebhardt's home, was set to be drilled.

Ben Coker, Marie Broder and the entire law enforcement protecting Griffin and Spalding County were nervous. Suspects had been arrested and were in jail, evidence was being gathered, but still the prosecution knew their key witnesses were a, "rogue's gallery," and were far less than 100% reliable. Drug dealers, thieves, drunks and a child molester were all ready to take the stand. The idea of using Atlanta HydroVac drilling the well next to Gebhardt's house, was a viable one, one that just might turn up the evidence they needed for solid conviction.

However, the lack of physical evidence had worried the prosecutors from the start.

Coker and his team met the day before with Judge Scott Ballard in his Fayetteville office requesting the search warrant to drill the well. A search warrant was issued. GBI Agent Coleman had received information from multiple sources that Gebhardt had thrown evidence from the murder down his well. Armed with the search warrant the team would begin to search the house on Patterson.

Christina Froehlich Kannon, GBI Forensic Expert, took photographs in and around the house. Some 60-70 knives were found inside the drawers of the kitchen. One knife, Kannon would later testify, was similar to the one found at the bottom of the well. But the real evidence, prosecutors continued to believe was at the bottom of that well.

Drilling for water has been going on hundreds of years in America. Available water, with what use to be found with "divining rods," is now located with seismometers and graphs. Modern equipment then drills a hole into the ground and water, hopefully lots of it, is available to the homeowner. Traditional methods were not able to be used at the Patterson Road property. These methods call for three feet width be allowed for every foot drilled. This is due to the fact any less will compromise the ground surrounding the well. Gebhardt's home was so close to the dry well any traditional drilling method would be impossible.

With a promise of the well drilling hydrovac method provided, the prosecution now had a reasonable alternative. Greg Dubin owner of Atlanta HydroVac was contracted to do the work.

The company arrived early at Gebhardt's property on Patterson Road to begin their work. The property has three wells. The one next to the home in which Frankie lived was the well the investigators were interested in.

When Gebhardt's mother, Evelyn died, she deeded the property over to Sandra Bunn, Frankie's older sister. Sandra let Frankie live there, but the arrangement had been strained at times. Sandra once had to evict her brother taking him to court, case 03-D-0211, in 2003, due to non-payment (of rent). Bunn was awarded a default judgement on January 29, 2003 in the Spalding County Magistrate Court. Since that time Bunn had deeded the property over to her son, Lamar.

The system of recovering items using the hydrovac method is much like that of a shop vac and pressure washer. A pressure wash type system is used to begin and expand a hole in the ground. A vacuum system will then suck the water, and any items, back out of the hole into a large tanker truck. The truck will subsequently be driven to an area where a large collection tarp is then placed on the ground and the contents emptied. This was the first time any prosecution team in Georgia would use this method to find acceptable evidence which could be entered into court records. But the drilling was still a risky proposal. What if evidence, the prosecution hoped would be there, was not found?

Thursday, April 12, 2018

The hydrovac team began to use a pressure wash type device to "round out," the well. This took time. Assistant District Attorney Marie Broder knew it would be the turning point if evidence was found in the well.

The digging and excavation would be an all-day event

Deeper the drillers went

Five feet…seven feet…ten feet…deeper and deeper the workers dug.

A crowd began to gather, mostly comprised of Gebhardt's and some of Moore's family members. Lawn chairs were set up. Lunch brought out. It was like a carnival, the fair. Family members were certain there was nothing in that well. Frankie had told them so.

All the while the crowd watched the drill go lower and lower and lower.

It would take a total of 10 hours for the workmen to flush out the well. The team had to drill, suck out and empty the tanker truck before the evidence could be sifted through. The DA's office knew that any DNA evidence could be destroyed by the high-pressure water going down the hole. This had been confirmed by James Sebestyen, a GBI Forensic Biologist. "Pressure washing is not a good thing (for evidence). Items would be mostly compromised," and DNA would not be able to be used.

But why was DNA so important.

DeoxyriboNucleic Acid (DNA) is a unique structure of cells within everyone's body. Discovered by a Swiss medical student, Johann Friedrich Miescher in 1868, it would not be used on a routine basis in the United States until 1990.

Ashley Hinkle, a Forensic Biologist for the GBI Crime Lab would later testify that her duties were to test evidence items for bodily fluid(s) and compare the DNA profiles. Hinkle works up to 400 cases a year and had given her expert testimony at over 130 trials. DNA is within everyone's body. Hinkle compares known samples to unknown samples to see if there are matches.

Investigators turn to the FBI CODIS Database where DNA evidence is stored. Law enforcement agencies from around the nation can compare DNA evidence gathered from convicted offenders and unsolved crime scenes to see if there is a match. Another part of the database is the National DNA Index System, or NDIS which contains the DNA contributed by federal, state and local forensic labs.

But there were two problems with drilling the well:

1) Any evidence the prosecution might find would be 34 plus years old;

2) Pressure from the water used in the drilling could compromise blood samples found.

Drilling came to a stop. The water and sludge from the well had been sucked out. But was there any evidence or items left at the bottom of the well? Was there anything left to collect?

Frankie Gebhardt knew about the drilling and sat in his jail cell trying to persuade himself nothing would be found. Again, and again Gebhardt tried to convince himself the folly the law enforcement was having drilling his well. The murderer well knew when he threw the chain, the clothing, the knife down the well it would never be found. When he burned trash in that same well it would surely destroy what he had discarded so long ago.

The drilling was big news. Television stations from Atlanta recorded clips of the event for their evening newscasts.

Terry Reed was incarcerated (probation violation) in the Spalding County jail when the drilling news came on tv. Gebhardt and Reed were friends. They had even been in the same cell together. Reed and other inmates had heard Frankie talking and when the group saw the news on the television they rallied to watch. "We were out cleaning up the tables when the news came on the tv," Reed would remember. "Frankie had told me they were not going to find any DNA evidence in that well. He told me they took 61 knives from his property." But Reed would come to the aid of this new-found friend when he said, "Everyone in jail was talking about it (the murder, the well drilling, the investigation). I didn't listen to nobody but Frankie."

Reed would soon find he too had been duped by his, "friend," Frankie.

Coker, Dix, Broder and Coleman all speculated; would they ever get this evidence to the top? From the back of the group came a voice volunteering to go to the bottom. The group was both astounded and relieved. One of the workers from Atlanta HydroVac volunteered to go to the bottom. Luckily the fire department was on the scene and had inspected the drilled area. They determined it was safe to go, as long as safety precautions and protective clothing was worn by the worker.

To this day the worker who headed down that long, dark shaft refuses to be identified.*** But he and others know, he is the unsung hero of this 34-year old case. Unknown to Gebhardt at the time, what he had thrown down the well with the intention of destroying actually helped preserve the evidence. The trash, the cans, the old stuff Frankie had thrown down had acted as a buffer in the cold, damp, dank water well. When he had burned his trash, it only provided an extra layer of carbon to protect the evidence.

With safety protection, a bucket and a headlamp, the worker was carefully lowered into the well, inch by precious inch.

The well smelled from the sludge sucked to the top. It was dark and dank. Only a hole of light could be seen at the top.

Inch by inch…lower…ever lower.

For the anxious crowd, untold minutes passed. Then the unsung hero reached the bottom of the well. With his gloved hands the worker felt around. He touched something that felt like metal. It was a chain, links larger than usual. With light shining toward the bottom, the hero would then notice a rusted-out knife handle with two nearby blades. He placed these items in the bucket.

Lying in the well he saw and collected several other items. These items felt like clothes, covered with the muddy red clay from the dried-up water well. Into the bucket they went.

The worker then motioned he wanted to head back to the top. With that the wrench began its work. The worker and the bucket came to the top, a little quicker than they had gone down.

A wave of cheers met the worker as his helmet crested the top of the well. Not sure of what had been found Coker and his team went toward the bucket. Gloves were put on so as not to contaminate whatever evidence there might be.

What a glorious sight. There in plain sight, in the bucket was a chain, some clothing caked in red clay mud and what appeared to be several knife blades.

Prosecution had struck gold!

What the unsung hero had brought to the top was indeed "the silver chalice," find for the prosecutors. Although Gebhardt didn't know it, the lucky find would cost him plenty. It might even cost him his freedom.

The tanker truck was driven to the Spalding County Jail complex. It went behind the building and began to empty the contents onto a large black plastic collection tarp. It was getting dark. The area would have to be secured for the night before investigators could sift through the sludgy contents.

Two deputies were posted overnight. No one would get into this half football field evidence zone.

From inside the prison walls, Gebhardt could see the tanker truck back up, dispose of its contents and the sheriff cars entering and exiting the area. He knew they had found something. Gebhardt's mind began to race, "Could it be…Nah that shit is burned up," The sun began to set in the west beyond the highway bypass, named in honor of Dr. Martin Luther King, Jr. "Nah…they ain't found shit," he tried to convince himself.

But better safe than sorry Frankie would call his sister, Sandra, that night. She could take care of this. She always took care of him. He was her baby brother. Sandra had always gotten him out of trouble.

As the deputies stood guard over the evidence, the group of prosecutors and lawmen could hardly sleep that night. It would be an early morning, sifting through the discharge of the tanker.

Assistant District Attorney Marie Broder went to sleep that night smiling her southern smile thinking, "We got him. We got him for sure."

Friday, April 13, 2018, early morning
back of the Spalding County Sheriff's Office

Prosecutors had indeed hit a gold mine of evidence.

Items would be cleaned and examined by another expert, Daniella Stuart, GBI Special Agent and Crime Scene Specialist. Not only would Stuart look over the items from the well, she would see if she could find some of the missing evidence. She did find a rock that had been found at the murder scene with blood stains on it. But the missing club, the bottle of Jack Daniel's Whiskey, the cast of the tire tracks, all lost.

Broder and Coker could hardly contain their excitement. Item by item was laid out on a table. Carefully, every careful, investigators would look over the evidence from the tanker truck and bucket.

Found:

-A larger than normal chain, could have been used with a logging or pulp-wooding operation;

-A red Argyle sock, the kind Coggins might have worn, not a burly man like Gebhardt;

-A rusty knife handle with two blades, similar to the ones found inside Gebhardt's house;

-A shirt that had been burned with seven, what appeared cut, holes on the outside;

-A tennis shoe.

Unknown at the time the most important evidence found that day that would be relevant to the trial would be that shoe. An old, what had once been white, tennis shoe. Timothy Coggins body had been found without socks or shoes. When pulled from the well, the shoe, with the shirt and socks, were caked with red mud, sooty materials. But when cleaned up the prosecution knew they had, "THE," find. This was evidence that would link Gebhardt to the murder.

When investigators looked on the internet, they discovered this particular shoe was an Adidas, size 10 shoe. The exact kind and size Timothy wore in 1983. When she was later shown the shoe, Timothy's sister Telisa began to cry. That was the shoe. "It was my Timothy's shoe."

Investigators knew without a doubt they had Gebhardt now. Gebhardt was indeed one of the murderers. As they had been informed by those who were scared to testify before, Frankie had thrown clothing, a logging chain, a knife and this shoe down the well to burn and try and destroy evidence.

This was the evidence the District Attorney, Sheriff, the GBI had been looking for. It sure beat their list of incarcerated witnesses!

This was the evidence Christopher Joseph Vaughn shared when Frankie had bragged to him in that jail cell, saying, "I threw that n------- stuff down the well after we killed him."

"There had been so many obstacles to this case," Marie Broder thought to herself. "So many obstacles along the way to solving this 34-year old cold case."

These items, the shoe, the clothes, the knife, the chain, found at the bottom of that dried out well…these were the items that would be the keys to solving a somewhat shaky case.

Only a jury could decide, but the assistant district attorney left the field that day with a renewed and transformed confidence. She was going to win this case. She was definitely going to win this 34-year old unsolved cold murder case.

Broder remembered the lessons she had learned in school, in Sunday school. The lessons from her parents that she could be anybody and accomplish anything she wanted. But most of all Marie Broder remembered her grandfather, Arlis Burch, and their visit those many years ago. It was then she learned about injustice and the light sentence the murderer of her grandfather's brother received. It was on that day the young girl decided to become a prosecuting attorney. No, Timothy Wayne Coggins had not died because he was, "just another black man." His murderer would receive the full punishment he deserved.

Justice would be served after 34 long years.

Marie Broder was going to make sure of that.

Chapter 12
Conscience and consequences

*"Take the time to deliberate, but when the time for action
has arrived, stop thinking and go in (to battle)."*
Napoleon Bonaparte

April-June 2018, Another flurry of motions before the trial

- On April 25, 2018, Larkin Lee and Scott Johnston quickly moved with a petition and motion to suppress this evidence in court. The defense argued in the seven- page petition that the original warrant filed against their client Gebhardt made no mention of "searching a well on his property, nor that the well be dug up and searched." Judge Sams would *deny* the motion several weeks later in May.

- Several motions were filed on May 17, 2018, that asked evidence and testimony from Ruth Guy and Casey Moore be expelled and not used in court. Both Guy and (Casey) Moore had died. Guy had allegedly been a girlfriend of Gebhardt and had witnessed the murder. Casey Moore had allegedly told investigators that Gebhardt was doing repair work at his house and had stayed there both Thursday, October 6, and again Saturday, October

8, 1983. *The motion was allowed.* Guy's and (Casey) Moore's testimony nor hearsay would be used.

- May 31, 2018, the mental evaluation report on Franklin George Gebhardt was received by the Spalding County Clerk of Court for its records and was sealed by Judge Sams. The outside, "sealing order," showed that Gebhardt was evaluated "competent," to stand trial.

- In a last-ditch effort to disallow testimony from the prosecution witnesses, Scott Johnston, one of Gebhardt's defense attorneys, made a motion on June 1, 2018, that asked the court to consider testimony from five of the witnesses, who had felony records, not be allowed to testify. This included in what previously had been the prosecution's key witness, child molester, Christopher Joseph Vaughn. *The motion was denied* and the five would be allowed to testify at the trial.

- The state would have one more motion which asked that two felony offenses by Gebhardt be considered for punishment if he was convicted. Both were "Aggravated Assault," one from 1997, and the other from 2003. *The motion was allowed.*

- Due to the media coverage from local, state, national and even international media, Judge Sams ruled that two video cameras and a still camera be allowed in the courtroom. He also ruled that no video or photograph of Gebhardt in handcuffs or shackles be released prior to the verdict. No photograph or video of any juror was to be taken or released nor any witness interviewed by the media unless released by a resolution of the court.

  Judge Sams was going to have an orderly, respectful courtroom during the trial.

- Bill Moore would continue to wait in his jail cell. His attorney, Harry Charles filing no motions on his behalf. His trial would be held after Gebhardt's.

Monday, June 18, 2018

The day had finally arrived. Both sides, the prosecution and defense were ready, "to go into battle." The Spalding County Courthouse would open at 8 a.m. Some 30-40 interested citizens, potential jurors, family members of both the victim and accused were already lined up at

7:30 a.m. It was hot and humid, even for the morning hours, in Griffin, GA. Temperatures would soar to 92 degrees, the hottest of the year so far, when the trial began.

Three trials were set to begin this day. Gebhardt's trial would take place on the third floor of the courthouse. Gebhardt's legal defense team had successfully "severed," their trial away from that of co-accused, Bill Moore. But the defense team was disappointed they had not gotten a venue change or suppressed the evidence found in the dry well. After all the preliminaries, the motions, the procedures, Franklin George Gebhardt's trial was ready begin. Moore would have to wait until later that summer in August.

Bailiff William Matchett exclaimed, "All rise. The honorable Judge W. Fletcher Sams presiding." With that Judge Sams came out of his chambers and sat in his chair at exactly 9 a.m. Sams is a stickler for precision in his courtroom. The preliminaries had taken place, the jury had been chosen and court case 18-R-105A was ready to begin. A flurry of activity surrounded the courthouse that morning. A total of 325 citizens of Spalding County had been summoned to appear for one of three trials taking place. Judge Sams was notified that only 127 cared to show up. Judge Sams wasn't happy with the lack of attendance by the potential jurors and ordered the Spalding Sheriff's Office to, "find the missing individuals and bring them to my court," when things settled down and they could send patrol cars out to round up those called.

Sams would immediately delay the anticipated beginning of the trial until 10:45 a.m. due to the shortage of personnel from the sheriff's office to handle the volume of cases going on. Security was tight, not only for the Gebhardt trial but also for a rival gang related trial taking place a floor below.

It was a good thing Judge Sams had delayed the start of the Gebhardt trial. Gebhardt had been incarcerated for 14 months awaiting trial for sexual battery prior to his arrest in October 2017, for murder. Gebhardt had gained a tremendous amount of weight, during his lifetime of crime, but particularly putting on the pounds during his recent incarceration. During trials, defendants can wear, "regular clothes." The accused do not have to wear prison stripes. Gebhardt's "regular clothes" did not fit. In fact, when she saw him for the first time in months, Gebhardt's niece, Brandy Abercrombie pointed out, "Uncle Frankie's done got fat!" And he had. The delay gave the defense team time to get "clothes that fit," onto Frankie.

Franklin George Gebhardt, the accused murderer, sat at the defense bench, left of Judge Sams, bald head, grey goatee, light blue shirt, dark sports coat and dark pants, "that fit."

Tuesday, June 19, 2018

Preliminaries and jury selection would take the better part of the first two days. By Tuesday afternoon, June 19, 2018, a jury had been selected. It was a cross section of Spalding County. All walks of life; black, white, all ages, all type occupations. Judge Sams called the chosen 15 (12 jurors and 3 alternates) back into the courtroom. The panel of 9 white females, 1 African American female, 4 white males and 1 African American male took their seats near the witness stand, to the right of Judge Sams and to the side of the prosecution table. They were given instructions to return the following morning for the beginning of the trial. They were not to discuss with anyone, family, friends, no one about the trial or their involvement.

Wednesday, June 20, 2018

On the right side of Judge Sams was the prosecuting team; Ben Coker, Marie Broder, Jared Coleman, Mike Morris and Investigator John Wright.

On Judge Sams' left was the defense team; Larkin Lee, Scott Johnston, Frankie Gebhardt, Brent Hutchinson and Bill Moore's attorney Harry Charles. Moore was not in the courtroom since his trial had been severed from that of his brother-in-law Frankie Gebhardt.

Inside the packed courtroom were both members of the Coggins family, a united front of about 30 family members who were in the courtroom every day of the trial; and 7-10 members of the Gebhardt and Moore families. With general matters settled, the audience became somber as the twelve jury members and three alternates jury were led into the courtroom at 9:11 a.m.

That's the American way.

That's how democracy works.

It ain't pretty but it works!

"Mrs. Broder," Judge Sams said looking toward the assistant district attorney. "You may begin your opening statement."

Prosecution opening statement

As noted, crime novelist, Dominick Dunne, wrote, "female prosecutors must be tough. Jurors, even though they want to be fair and unopinionated, are basically sexist.

*They do not like strong female attorneys, even if their job
was to put rapists and murders behind bars."*

Marie Broder, Spalding County Assistant District
Attorney, is that tough as nails prosecuting attorney.

District Attorney Ben Coker had put his trust in Broder.
She would be the lead attorney in trying the case. The
win, or loss was to be hers. She owned this one. This
was not, however, Broder's first, "big" case. Out of 30
previous murder trials, 10 of the accused had been
sentenced to life in prison. But there is always this one
time, she thought. In what appeared to be a calmness on
the outside Broder was visibly nervous as Judge Sams
called her name.

Marie Broder thanked the judge and began her
statement. "When a victim is killed, murdered, that victim
cannot take the stand and tell you what happened. This
crime scene where an unspeakable crime occurred…it
whispers to you as to what happened," Broder softly
spoke to the jury.

She then spoke louder, "And sometimes it screams. The
field off Minter Road became a killing field. (The field)
screams to you, (to find justice)." Broder described the
lacerations and abrasions, "so many they could not be
counted," Coggins had all over his body. "You will hear

the crime scene (of a 23-year old man who was murdered) SCREAM. Listen to it. Listen to it," Broder urged.

The prosecutor would then go on to describe how the crime had occurred 34 years ago. About how a young man, at the beginning of his life was, "brutally murdered." How he had attended a club to have a good time. How he had ended up at Carey's and was seen arguing. "A few hours later he would die."

How Gebhardt and Moore had tied Coggins feet to the back of a truck and drug the body through the field. How they stabbed Coggins multiple times.

Broder did acknowledge the initial investigation by the county and state was, "incomplete and shameful. They simply did not care about Timothy Coggins." She noted how items gathered at the initial crime scene, the red sweater, the plaster of Paris tire track casts, the bottle of Jack Daniel's Whiskey, had been lost or destroyed. "But, the one thing I can tell you, Bill Moore's day in court will come, but this man's day in court is TODAY," Broder said pointing to Frankie Gebhardt. The accused sat unemotional and still, staring ahead with his cold black eyes.

"You…the jury…can atone for the sins of the past," Broder said thanking the jury and sitting down.

Defense opening statements

Scott Johnston, one of Gebhardt's two defense attorneys, would make his opening statements.
"Rage…anger…fury…the state wants you to hurry through this case. Just like in 1983, they want you to hurry through this case. They (county and state) had given up on it. It was, 'just another black man.'"

Johnston would then go on to describe how the state and county had botched the case in 1983 and why it was cold 34 years later. He would describe how evidence was lost or destroyed, how items were found at the bottom of Gebhardt's well. "The state will tell you it's a cold case…it is. BUT they (must) prove beyond a reasonable doubt, Frankie Gebhardt, (and later Moore,) are guilty. The state does not get a pass on this."

The defense attorney concluded his 14 minutes opening statement by saying, "Lots of folks will be saying things but listen who is saying these things. Ladies and gentlemen. This is a horrible thing that was done to this man (Coggins). I just want you to…what you are here to do decide is that these are the facts. Don't let anger or rage influence (you). Once you hear all this you *WILL* have reasonable doubt."

Of the 103 original witnesses, the state's prosecution would call a total of 24 witnesses to take the stand and testify in the trial before they closed their portion of the case. The defense, oddly enough, would call only two witnesses before they closed.

Monday, June 25, 2018, Closing arguments

Both the prosecution, represented by Ben Coker, and the defense, represented by Larkin Lee had memorable closing arguments.

Coker would begin his arguments by reminding jurors that, "the judge will charge you today with reasonable doubt. This does not mean that the state must prove each and every single thing. Across courtrooms across our country criminals will be convicted with far less evidence than what you have today."

Coker would conclude by pointing at Franklin George Gebhardt and saying, "One thing that has reigned through is that man right over there, is a racist and a killer of Timothy Wayne Coggins." Coker would take 45 minutes for his closing arguments.

Larkin Lee would then begin his arguments. Lee would continue to point out how, "evidence was lost," and that no one wanted evidence in this trial more, "than we do." Lee would then recap his testimony for the jurors. "Ladies and gentlemen, the witnesses the state has presented to you has less than ZERO credibility."

Lee would continue, "Three trained law officers matching wits with a man who has a sixth-grade education. Is he that much smarter than all those folks, or is he telling the truth when he says, 'I don't know a damn thing about it.'"

Concluding his hour and a half closing statement, Larkin Lee looked at the jury and asked, "It is difficult to put aside someone who uses racial slurs, who is mean. You must put that aside and find this man not guilty. You have to find him guilty BEYOND a reasonable doubt. Put the state to their burden (of proof) and make sure they show you the case beyond a reasonable doubt. And with that I thank you."

Lee went back to his defense table, exhausted.

In an ironic twist, storm clouds and thunder from the summers' heat began to roll into Griffin from the west just as Judge Sams was charging the jury with their instructions for deliberations. Judge Sams would ask the jury to select a foreperson once they were sequestered and asked them to have, "an open mind in this case." Again, the jury was cautioned by Judge Sams that they were "to talk to no one, read nothing, communicate with no one about this case." They were told to communicate with the judge only in writing. Lastly, under Georgia law, Sams reminded them, any decision would have to be unanimous.

The jury was handed the case at 4:04 p.m.

They would return an hour and fifteen minutes later, no decision had been made.

They were dismissed for the day.

+++++++

When filed with the records at the end of 2018, this case, the investigation, the hearings against Franklin George Gebhardt and William Franklin Moore, would be transcribed into over 11,000 pages, bound into seven volumes of gruesome and nauseating details of a shocking murder.

+++++++

Tuesday, June 26, 2018, A jury decides

It was the seventh day of the trial.

The jury continued their deliberation. No one knew how long it would take them to reach a decision.

During the time the court waited on the decision, Melanie Nichols and Christy Cornett, who worked with Judge Sams took care of paperwork. Nichols has worked with Judge Sams for 25 years, as he was in private practice, elected State Court Judge in 1996, and Superior Court Judge in 2010.

Gina Ritchie, the court reporter, reviewed the transcripts she was preparing.

Bailiffs Barbara Puerifoy, Jim Goolsby and William Matchett sat outside the jury room as they awaited word.

The defense team waited at their table while the prosecution retired to the district attorney's offices. Frankie Gebhardt would wait for word in a holding cell directly behind the courtroom.

The families of both Timothy Wayne Coggins and Franklin George Gebhardt waited inside and outside the courtroom.

Judy Baumann, an interested citizen, sat patiently in her seat, having attended each day of the trial, "because I'm interested in what goes on in Griffin."

Photographers, reporters, cameramen and women, television anchors compared notes, chatted and drank copious amounts of coffee.

The jury returns

At exactly 2:46 p.m. the jury sent a note to Judge Sams stating they were ready to announce their decision. It was time for their conscience and decision to declare the consequences, innocence or guilt, Franklin George Gebhardt's fate.

The courtroom filled once again. Everyone taking their seats. The cameramen, reporters and scribes were eager to record and relay the decision onto a waiting public. That hour was near.

At exactly 2:57 p.m. Judge Sams entered the courtroom and informed everyone a verdict had been reached. Judge Sams reminded all that he would not allow any emotional outburst, any cheering, any applause, any media running around. "If you cannot do this, leave now." No one left.

His courtroom would be dignified befitting a court of law.

"I do not know what the verdict is. I respect their decision. This will be dealt with, with dignity and respect. I know it is a highly charged case on both sides."

He then asked Bailiff Jim Goolsby to lead the jury back into the courtroom.

When the men and women of the jury were seated, Judge Sams asked the foreman if they had reached a decision. "We have," the young man said.

Bailiff Goolsby would then hand Judge Sams the piece of paper the jury had used.

Sams reviewed the verdict and announced.......

Chapter 13

The day of reckoning

Tuesday, June 26, 2018, 3:02 p.m.

Prosecuting attorneys say that there are two things they look for when a jury returns from their deliberations:

1) If the jury enters the courtroom when they are ready to announce their verdict and they will not make eye contact with the accused and are very somber, the defendant is guilty;
2) If they are smiling or looking at the accused, they will probably submit an acquittal to the judge.

The jury in the Gebhardt trial was not looking at Frankie.

Judge Sams reviewed the note from the jury for about a minute.

He then began to pronounce the verdict:

"Count 1, Malice Murder. Guilty.

Count 2, Felony Murder. Guilty.

Count 3, Aggravated Battery. Guilty.

Count 4, Aggravated Assault. Guilty.

Count 5, Concealing the Death of Another. Guilty."

The jury had done their job for the state. It had taken a courageous law enforcement team and unwavering jury to convict Franklin George Gebhardt of a repugnant murder committed 34 years ago. As demanded, no one in the courtroom showed emotion. Judge Sams had already sent Brandy Abercrombie, Gebhardt's niece to jail for contempt at the beginning of the trial.

It had taken the jury a little over 7 hours to decide Gebhardt's guilt.

Gebhardt, Lee and Johnston remained seated during the pronouncement. Gebhardt appeared to be incredulous as the five guilty verdicts were read, not believing what he was hearing.

Judge Sams then turned to the jury and thanked them for their service. He explained that if any one of them wanted to leave they were allowed. All remained seated in the jury box. Judge Sams said he would return in 10 minutes to sentence Gebhardt for his crimes. A 10-minute recess was taken.

The sentence stunned the courtroom

Judge Sams returned to a silent and stunned courtroom.

He would at this point allow Heather Coggins, spokeswoman for the family, to speak to Gebhardt before sentencing. Ms. Coggins took the podium next to the prosecution with tears running down her cheek. "We want to thank the jury, the State (of Georgia) GBI, Marie (Broder), Ben (Coker), Sheriff Dix. We can now go back to the grave and Tim can rest in peace. Thank you...thank you so very much."

Gebhardt stared straight ahead, no remorse...no guilt.

Sams would then note this was one of the most, "heinous crimes," he had ever judged.

"Franklin George Gebhardt, for the murder of Timothy Wayne Coggins, you are sentenced to life in prison, plus 30 years....to run consecutive. Bailiffs, handcuff Mr. Gebhardt."

With that the bailiffs and sheriff deputies moved toward the defense table and put handcuffs on the murderer.

Before he left the courtroom, Judge Sams looked at and addressed Franklin George Gebhardt. "Hopefully sir, you have stabbed your last victim."

Reporters and the photographer close enough to hear Gebhardt heard him say, "I ain't killed no f---ing n-----."

With that law enforcement would lead Gebhardt out of the courtroom to an awaiting Sheriff's car. He took the last steps of freedom he would ever enjoy as he was taken back to his cell at the Spalding County Detention Center.

At this point several of the jurors were crying. It was an emotional scene. Judge Sams would allow, as he had throughout the trial, the jury to leave the courtroom first and return to their cars. Bailiff Barbara Puerifoy would watch out the west window of the courtroom, the same window that had shown the approaching storm the day before, as the jurors got into and left in their cars and trucks. Puerifoy then notified Judge Sams all jurors had gotten to their vehicles "safely."

With that Judge Sams said, "Court dismissed."

The trial of the decade, if not the century inside the small middle Georgia town, had come to a close. Franklin George Gebhardt was going to be in prison, probably for the rest of his life. He had murdered a young African American man, 34 years ago. A murder he crowed and bragged about until the victim's day in court arrived.

As Judge Sams left the courtroom, the Coggins family members began to hug each other and cry tears of joy. They had been a united front until the end. These brave and courageous souls were not going to let the murder of their brother, their uncle, their nephew be the murder of, "just another black man." Atonement had been found for his murder.

As prosecutor Broder asked for in her opening statement, the jury had taken care of the reckoning.

Law enforcement, the district attorney's office, GBI investigators all posed with family members in the back of the courtroom for a group photograph.

Everyone was smiling.

Then came the "group hug." Members hoped it would never end.

Larkin Lee and Scott Johnston, the defense attorneys, sat at their bench in stunned silence.

Today, justice had been found inside the courtroom of the Spalding County Courthouse.

A long 34 years, 256 days and 9 hours had transpired.

Racial bias and anger had been ingrained and taught to the murderer years ago. This would never change.

But prejudice…while prejudice may have been learned by many in that courtroom long ago…that day…that very day, Tuesday, June 26, 2018, prejudice would change…improve…be altered forever.

It was a new day in Spalding County.

It was a new day in Griffin.

It was a new day in the hamlet of Sunnyside.

The extraordinary had just happened in these small, average, everyday communities in middle Georgia. Where good folks live and work to improve their community.

Now Timothy Wayne Coggins' life had meaning, a purpose, a goodness that had been taken from him and his family long, long ago. It was a new beginning for the victim, the family and the community.

Timothy had not been, "just another black man," who had been murdered and forgotten.

It had been years, too many years for sure in coming, but today justice had been found in that small Georgia courtroom, during a sultry summer afternoon.

Justice found in the hands of the jury, the hearts of a community and the justice of the Lord.

———

"Yet the Lord longs to be gracious to you; therefore, He will rise up to show you compassion. For the Lord is a God of justice. Blessed are all who wait for Him!"

Isaiah 30:18

———

Chapter 14
Hope is written in the future tense

An hour before sunset, Tuesday, June 26, 2018

The sun, a persistent sun, would be setting in about an hour. It was slowly losing its grip on yet another hot summer day in the small middle Georgia town. The African American church was like many in the area, a simple structure with a white steeple reaching upward toward a cloudless blue sky.

Tonight, would be like many that had passed before. Still, peaceful, dark. Only the nearby sounds of passing cars along the highway would break the silence. The smell of fresh cut grass would surround the desolate cemetery. To the back of the church lay the graves of many of the members, some marked, many still not.

In the far southeast corner of the burial ground, 624 feet from the church, lies the grave of a young African American male. It is the grave of a life taken far too early. Only 23 when he was murdered, Timothy Wayne Coggins lay in the red Georgia clay where the body had seen summers, fall, winters and spring all pass slowly by. For 34 years, 256 days his dead body had seen hot weather, cold weather, beautiful springs and breathtaking falls in Georgia. Most of these years with no identification the young man who lay below in the cold, damp earth.

But tonight.

Tonight, all would be different.

Different because Timothy Wayne Coggins and his family finally found peace. Two deer meandered out of the woods with their ears forward, guarding the grave, silently noticing the transformation this night would bring.

Many of the unmarked graves still would not find the peace or justice their neighbor Timothy had discovered only hours earlier. Other sites had marble headstones identifying the soul within the confines of its depths. Timothy Wayne Coggins too had been properly identified with a headstone since the last New Year's Eve when an old year promised a fresh start…a new beginning. The family once feared if ever identified their loved one's body would be dug up, the gravesite desecrated, defiled by savage beasts who called themselves men. Hadn't they suffered enough?

But not tonight.

No tonight was about to be unlike any other. The young man whose freedom had been taken away from him those many years ago could now rest and truly be free for the rest of the ages. Franklin George Gebhardt, the beast, the murderer, the anger filled racist, was sixty years old. He had been a young man too when he had killed Timothy Coggins. Now sick and ill, Gebhardt was a throwback to another time. His rage and venom silenced, now and forever, his freedom lost to the ages.

The dead now knew peace.

The living murderers would know no peace.

The slight summer breeze made the pine trees sway, ever scraping, ever moving, standing tall and vigilant. But if you listened, listened closely, you could hear the silence of the voices from the graveyard.

Ghosts do not cry, but they do cheer for one of their own.

Only a few days before a fearless prosecuting attorney promised that the, "evidence would shout," from that silent murdered warrior lying in the graveyard. Her promises were kept. The silence of the falling night shouted volumes of freedom, change. A new day was soon to come with the morning sunrise.

In the Fuller Chapel United Methodist Church graveyard, the bright orange rays of sunset were turning to grey. Walking toward their home was an older African American man and lady. The gentleman used a cane as he held on tight to the arm of his wife. They walked home past the church for about an eighth of a mile, turned right to reach their small home, an old tenement house, just off the highway, along a dirt street, to settle in for the night.

Another young man, also African American, followed closely behind. He too, heading home from a day's work in town as a cook, a greasy once white apron thrown over his shoulder. As simple and as plain as it was, down the road a bit was his home. The graveyard a familiar site on his journeys back and forth, to and from.

Simple.

Plain.

But now, somehow, a little different.

Respect.

Understanding.

Peace.

Prejudice changed, hopefully forever.

Perhaps life now would be a little better than before.

The murder of a young African American man had been rectified. The villain behind steel bars, for the rest of his life.

Nearby the white Zebulon United Methodist Church has its own graveyard. Most of the sites have fancy marble headstones etched with flowers, cherubs and words glorifying Jesus and God. The sign on the church welcomed a new pastor. She began her ministry there the Sunday before.

The small Georgia town, as most of the south, has seen tremendous changes since 1983. The small town now has a regional banking operations center within its city limits. Push buttons help change traffic lights from red to green as pedestrians cross the busy highway. There are coffee shops that charge three dollars for a cup of coffee and let you pick from the assortment of goodies that line a glass case. Antique shops, a barbecue restaurant, gas station and convenience store all along the square downtown area.

Good people, working to make their community better.

A sign was spotted between the black and white churches.

"Join the fight…Honor our Veterans…Protect these Monuments," the red sign harked to the passersby. Appearing on the plaque of the Georgia Southern Confederate Veterans Organization was a photograph of the original carving of Robert E. Lee, Stonewall Jackson and Jefferson Davis from nearby Stone Mountain, long ago a rally point for the Ku Klux Klan and other "white supremist, hate groups." The cardboard sign was fading and beginning to wither from recent afternoon summer thunderstorms. Commemorations asking for membership to a long forgotten wayward cause will continue to be placed in the red clay along the Georgia roads and highways. But now, the hatred, the anger, the rage has slowly been drowned out. Another time, another era, another errant and way of life changing hopefully forever.

The change has begun.

No...it is no longer 1953, 1963, 1973 or, especially, 1983. Today in a small middle Georgia courtroom, the cries of freedom had been heard. Justice had been found and served. The whispers are now the shouting voices of the freed souls of that southern graveyard echoing across the still acre of the Georgia pines.

The dark still night will bring forth a new day, then another, then another.

Even as the sunset's light faded, the sweet taste of freedom, a lingering sensation of justice from today would remain forever in the still of that stifling summer night.

Timothy Wayne Coggins' spirit and his graveyard friends all smiled.

The pages within the chapter of this nightmare had finally been turned.

Somehow things were different, now.

Very different, and would be, from now on.

An Epilogue
Just off the Interstate 177 miles away

Franklin George Gebhardt

Frankie Gebhardt is currently serving time in the Reidsville Georgia State Prison. He is inmate number 0000039998. Gebhardt is in prison today with some of the baddest of the bad in his new home at Reidsville. He was transported first to the state prison in nearby Jackson for evaluation and diagnostics. Then sent to his new home in Reidsville. Gebhardt is now in the custody of the State of Georgia and will be for the rest of his life.

Reidsville is the primary maximum-security facility in Georgia for the Georgia Department of Corrections. The prison can accommodate 1538 males who have been convicted of felonies. Reidsville was first opened in 1938 and has housed some of some of the most dangerous criminals in Georgia's history. It was the site of Georgia's death row and the electric chair until 1980. At that time death row and the electric chair was moved to the Georgia Diagnostic and Classification State Prison in Jackson. Georgia. Lethal injection is now used for Georgia executions.

As is his right under the laws of the State of Georgia, Gebhardt and his legal team have appealed the guilty decision and life in prison sentence.

On Thursday morning, Valentine's Day, February 14, 2019, Franklin George Gebhardt appeared back in the Spalding County courtroom for the first time since his sentence. The murderer sat in front of Judge W. Fletcher Sams with his defense team to file a motion for a new trial.

Sitting with a visibly nervous Gebhardt, defense attorneys Larkin Lee and Scott Johnston argued as to why their client should have the murder case retried.

Gebhardt was wheeled into the courtroom. According to a relative Gebhardt had broken his leg when he stepped into a hole playing ball in prison.

Defense attorneys Lee and Johnston submitted 15, "Enumerations of Defense," on behalf of their client. This included items the defense team thought had been mishandled in the June 2018 trial. Items ranging from how certain witnesses were not, "agents of the State (of Georgia)," to, "evidence introduced," were part of the list. Another point the defense attorneys brought forth during the retrial request was a recording by witness Christopher Vaughn when he was in the same cell as

Gebhardt. Lee and Johnston claimed law enforcement had coached Vaughn as to what information they wanted from Gebhardt.

Assistant District Attorney Marie Broder argued each, "Enumerated," point made by the defense for the state sharing that a retrial should not be granted. Broder pointed out to Judge Sams that the state had carefully evaluated each piece of evidence presented and had solid legal case study behind each witness they brought to the stand.

During the hearing, Gebhardt, who was transported from Reidsville to Griffin, continued to nervously shake his right leg. He made no comments to the judge, and only discussed a couple of items with his attorney Lee.

Judge Sams asked both the state and defense to submit briefs to him within 10 days answering certain questions he requested from the "Enumerations." The defense had earlier submitted to Judge Sams and the state the 15 items citing the need for a retrial.

Judge Sams has reviewed these items and ruled a retrial was not necessary (May 30, 2019). The case has moved up the ladder so to speak and defense attorneys have asked the Georgia Supreme Court to consider their arguments. Murder cases do not go through the state appellate court system but rather are sent directly to the top court. This is where the case now resides, with the Georgia Supreme Court (September 17, 2019).

If the Georgia Supreme Court denies such a request, the defense could then submit their motion to the federal level of courts which could lead directly to the United States Supreme Court. The U.S. Supreme Court is the end of the line for any and all legal motions, files or requests. The full legal process could take years before coming to an end.

Unless overturned, Gebhardt is not eligible for parole since he has been given a life sentence for the murder of Timothy Wayne Coggins.

Franklin George Gebhardt will die in prison.

As the February 2019, 26-minute hearing ended, Gebhardt was wheeled from the courtroom back into custody of the Spalding County Sheriff's office. He was then transported back to Reidsville.

Franklin George Gebhardt has been allowed the last day of freedom he will ever enjoy.

He will never revisit the hamlet where he grew up or terrorize a community of honest, hard-working people.

Unless a retrial is granted by the State of Georgia or a Federal Judge, Franklin George Gebhardt will die alone in his small prison cell, 177 miles southeast from where he murdered a young 23-year-old African American man that chilly October night. It was a different time, a different era, those long, long years ago.

Timothy Wayne Coggins will long be remembered.

Franklin George Gebhardt will soon be forgotten.

For you see in the end goodness will triumph over evil, each, and every time.

-30-

Afterwards and updates

William Franklin Moore, Sr.

Bill Moore would wait 51 days after his brother-in-law Frankie Gebhardt had been found guilty to enter his plea into the court.

Moore's trial date was set for Thursday, August 16, 2018.

The district attorney, Coggins family, and Moore's attorney, Harry Charles, worked out a plea deal. Assistant District Attorney Marie Broder met with the Coggins family prior to entering the courtroom. Family members did not want to allow the deal unless Moore pled guilty to killing Timothy. Behind closed doors, Broder asked family members, "Let's close this chapter." She pointed out another trial, in which they would hear witnesses again describe the horrendous murder, could be devastating to the family.

Heather Coggins, family spokeslady, looked around the room. All agreed. It had been a long 34 plus years.

Moore was wheeled into the courtroom in a wheelchair. He did not look well. He was a sick man whose complexion was gray. Harry Charles sat with Moore at the defense table. The Spalding County District Attorney's office took their places at the prosecution bench. They had already notified Judge Sams of the plea arrangement.

Today was plea day in the Spalding County Courthouse. Judge Sams would spend the day listening to pleas from accused and their attorneys that filled his third-floor courtroom. No jurors were seated in the jury box.

Judge Sams entered and asked everyone to be seated.

The first case he would listen to first was 18-R-105B, State of Georgia vs. William Franklin Moore. Judge Sams looked at the prosecution and defense and said he understood a plea arrangement had been worked out. Moore's defense attorney Harry Charles rose and said yes. Broder rose and said they had, and that the family agreed with the plea.

Judge Sams would then speak from his bench. "The only reason I am accepting this is because of (your) lawyer and the law enforcement recommends (it). I do not like it."

With that Judge Sams sentenced William Franklin Moore, Sr. to 20 years in prison followed by 10 years supervised probation. Sams had wanted to sentence Moore to additional time in prison, perhaps life in prison as his friend Gebhardt had been sentenced. But this was the plea and Judge Sams accepted it.

Moore sat in front of the judge in his wheelchair in his blue prison overalls and white sweatshirt underneath. Harry Charles, his attorney, stood at the podium. Judge Sams allowed Heather Coggins, Timothy's niece and spokeslady for the family to say what she wanted to Moore. As Heather came to the podium, the young lady spoke loud and clear. "What you did to our family…it tore our family apart. This has been a long time coming. We finally have some closure. We forgive you (Moore) for what you did to our family. I hope whoever you pray to, forgives you too."

With that Heather returned to her seat with her family members, still the 30 strong in attendance as they had been for Gebhardt's entire trial. As she dried her tears, Moore continued to stare at the floor in front of the judge. Repentant, as he had appeared in the first hearing in front of Magistrate Judge Rita Cavanaugh, November 2017.

Only the Lord and Bill Moore know if his repentance is sincere.

"You are dismissed," Judge Sams said as he took a short recess to allow those attending the murder plea to leave.

Moore was wheeled out of the courtroom, to return to the Spalding County jail and then to the Diagnostic and Classification State Prison located in nearby Jackson, GA for placement within the penal system.

Ben Coker, Spalding County District Attorney met with reporters after the plea hearing. "Today marks the end of a long road and arduous journey for the family of Timothy Coggins. My heartfelt thanks goes out to law enforcement for their work on this case. May Timothy rest in peace and may his family begin to heal."

Bill Moore is currently an inmate, number 0000591750, in the Georgia Penal System at the Johnson State Prison located in Wrightsville, GA. His jail term will end in July 2038. Moore will be 79 years old and will face another 10 years of supervised probation.

Brandy Abercrombie

Brandy Abercrombie, who is the niece of Gebhardt, was released from prison for contempt of court. She was allowed to attend the plea hearing of her father, Bill Moore. Abercrombie was so moved by the events of the day, once her father had been sentenced and the courtroom recessed, Brandy headed outside and found Heather Coggins and her family in front of reporters. She immediately began hugging family members, who began hugging her back. "I'm sorry," she said. "I'm so very sorry."

"We forgive you," Heather Coggins cried.

Abercrombie's father and brother are both in jail for murder. Her mother, Brenda, Frankie's baby sister and Bill Moore's wife, is dead. Brandy returned to her husband and child a different person. One filled with love. A prejudice changed.

Christopher Joseph Vaughn

Christopher Vaughn currently resides in the Riverbend Correctional Facility in Milledgeville, GA. and is inmate number 0000786186.

Vaughn committed the acts of Child Molestation for which he was imprisoned in 2004. He was 31 years old.
Vaughn will be eligible for parole in 2054. He will be 81 years old.
He is still waiting on that call to take time off his sentence for helping.

The Coggins Family

Members of the Timothy Wayne Coggins family now

were able to go about their daily lives in a more routine way. While never forgetting their loved one, Timothy, the family has a feeling of relief and justice served. They continue to praise the lawmen and women who helped solve the 34-year old cold murder case.

And from time to time, each visit Tim's grave, place flowers, say prayers. Especially on New Year's Eve.

Timothy Wayne Coggins

A young man who was so viciously killed those many years ago lies in his now marked grave at the Faith Chapel United Methodist Church in Zebulon. His spirit has seen the hot summer days pass, the cold winter snow come, and spring flowers bloom in the once pasture that is now a graveyard.

Oh, and the two deer. They can be seen time and again at the gravesite bringing their little ones, a young buck and a young doe. The young ones sniff the Georgia red clay, hunting for acorns while their parents stand in silent vigilance, remembering the somber days past and the glorious days ahead.

Life.

Death.

Courage.

Change.

Especially change.

They are really all the same.

OQMIII

An Interview with William Franklin Moore, Sr.

Thursday, February 21, 2019
Johnson State Prison
Wrightsville, GA

The driver headed south into desolate land. This was the other Georgia. A forgotten area where jobs are scarce, but pine trees and kaolin mines abound.

One-hundred ten miles southeast of Griffin and Spalding County lies the Johnson State Prison in Wrightsville, GA. The community is mostly known as the home of famous UGA football running back, Herschel Walker. Johnson State Prison is the only facility that offers, "good paying," jobs for the people of the area. This is a 1600 inmate, 300 staff, medium security prison within the State of Georgia penal system.

The area is isolated…to say the least.

But this is where William Franklin Moore is in prison. Moore agreed to an interview which was held February 21, 2019. Thanks to the Georgia Department of Corrections, Joan Heath and Marcus Floyd, the author was granted a one time, one-hour interview with the man who pled guilty to the murder of Timothy Wayne Coggins.

Visitors are led through a series of locked then unlocked doors, through gates with barbed razor wire across the top of chain link fences. Even though it is a medium security Georgia prison, unlike the maximum-security environs of Reidsville where Franklin George Gebhardt is imprisoned, there is no easy escape into the environs around this prison.

A quality rehabilitation program is offered to prisoners at the facility in the hopes their lives will be changed forever.

Bill Moore's life has certainly changed. While no stranger to the penal system of Georgia, Moore entered the prison a very sick man. When he was wheeled into the Spalding County courtroom that August 2018 day to enter a plea of guilty, many attending did not expect him to live out the year.

It's hard to fathom, but Moore is better off inside the prison than outside. He looked alive, healthy and the gray chalky complexion is gone, thanks to the medical attention he is receiving while incarcerated.

The author had one hour with a lifetime of questions to ask. Moore had a lifetime to talk about with only an hour to remember. Thus, the interview began.

Melton   "Bill thank you for agreeing to this interview. This is a great chance for you to clear the air about

William Franklin Moore…what happened (with your life and murder of Timothy Wayne Coggins). There is a lot of talk in Griffin, a lot of junk being said. This is your chance to clear it all up."

Moore   "Thank you Mr. Quimby for coming. I'm interested in what's going on and what people are saying. This is something right here I don't know nothing about anyway. Honestly, I don't know nothing about this (the murder)."

Why did you plead guilty?

Melton   "Why did you plead guilty?"

Moore   "I did what I did (pled guilty) to keep from winding up with more time (like Gebhardt who received life in prison). When I got to court, the only reason I did what I did…see I had that lawyer, that little lawyer (reminded Moore his lawyer's name was Harry Charles defense attorney for the state)…yeah Harry Charles. The only reason I did what I did I kindda went with the recommendation he led me toward. So, I knowed what they had done to Frankie."

Melton   "You knew ahead of time (before he pled guilty) what they (the court) had done to Frankie?"

Moore   "I knew ahead of time what they'd done to that boy. Because I couldn't stand the thought…the idea of facing a life in prison Mr. Quimby. I had no reason to hold anything back. I said nothing more than what I told my family (and lawyer). I told my lawyer I don't know nothing more about this. To this day, you know, I don't understand why me! I ain't done nothing."

Moore has no money. He relied on the state's attorneys to defend him in court. On the other hand, as mentioned above in the book, Gebhardt has relatives paying for his defense team.

Melton   "Do you think your lawyer, Harry Charles, did a good job?"

Moore   "Well. I think he done the best he thought he could do because he knew what they had done to Frankie."

Attorney Charles was at the June 2018 Gebhardt trial every day, sitting on the defense team side.

Moore   "And he (would have had) a tough time trying to convince a jury I was not guilty. Based on what everybody is telling everybody. (They say) so many people know so much about me. How do they know? Question somebody who knows something about it…not folks who don't know nothing about it. I don't want people hating on me (like they are). I was born and raised in that so-called place (Sunnyside). I still have a chance for parole. I'm looking to get out of here. I'm not looking to spending the rest of my life in this place."

Moore was sentenced to 20 years in prison with 10 years parole to follow. It will be 2037 if he serves his entire sentence. Moore would be approximately 78 years old.

Melton   "There is a lot of talk that you and your lawyer (Harry Charles) made a deal for you to tell everything (and publish in a book). I don't know if this is real or fake.

Moore   "No sir, there is no truth to that."

Frankie the, "bad ass"

Melton   "Let's go back to 1983 (the year of the murder). Tell me what happened."

Moore   "Mr. Quimby, in 1983 I was a pulp-wooder, a roofer, really a jack of all trades. First, I ever heard about all this (the murder) was six weeks prior to my arrest (2018). They come to my house questioning me about all kind of things you know about this here situation. About do I know this Coggins fellow? I don't know this Coggins fellow. I never met a Mr. Coggins.

"Frankie is the kind of fellow who always wants to build himself up. He always wanted to make himself to look like a bad ass. Pardon my French. Frankie always drug my name in(to) anything he could think of to build himself up. This is how my name got involved in this situation. As far as what Frankie has done all his life, I can't answer that Mr. Quimby. Cause I don't know I didn't marry that boy (read below how Moore dated and later married Frankie's sister, Brenda).

"You know, I've worked with him (Gebhardt) and he's worked with me. We've always been best boys and all this. But I've never heard Frankie talk about any of this."

Moore would then begin crying.

Moore   "The people of Griffin who don't even know me…I've always tried to be the best person I could be…I ain't done any of this. Frankie has gotten himself into a pickle. He (Frankie) got himself into a bad situation. He's about drove his sister (Sandra Bunn) crazy."

Moore would then stop talking to sob and visibly shake. He would continue about a minute then recover.

Moore   "It's like this Mr. Quimby. Frankie's done got me in a pickle. Honestly, if I knew about this case or what happened I could see why I was here. But for the life of me I don't (understand). I pray every day and night to help me remember if I had anything to do with this.

Moore   "Come on now…from 1983…(people) come up and make these accusations. Come on now. If I had done something like this I could not live with myself. If I had killed somebody, I would have known it."

At this point Moore would let out a big sigh…a lot of emotion lifting from his chest.

Moore would then go on to talk about how he knew that Gebhardt had begun his retrial request in court, appearing before Judge Sams in Spalding County, February 14, 2019. He also knew that a story was going around that Gebhardt had broken his leg.

Moore understood that Gebhardt was very nervous during the retrial motion hearing.

Moore   "Yes sir, that's what I understand."

Melton   "Were you and Frankie long time, friends?"

Moore   "I first got to know Frankie when I met his little sister (Brenda). I was about 16 years old (Brenda was 15). As far as me and Frankie being real close friends…we weren't at first. It was something that kind of grew on you (after I met his sister)."

Melton   "It's crazy that Frankie would bring your name up and try to get you in trouble if he likes you. He's not mad at you for marrying his sister, is he?

Moore   "No sir. His sister (Moore's wife Brenda) passed away shortly before all this stuff (Coggins murder) happened. I believe if she (Brenda) was alive today she would say that I am innocent. All my witnesses are gone (dead). I'm kindda having to fight this alone. You know what I mean?"

Moore would then go on to talk about his wife Brenda and their married life.

Moore   "Brenda always wanted to do the right thing. We, me and Brenda, got together (married) I was 17 and she was 16."

The couple would have a daughter, Brandy and later a son, William, Jr. Moore would then begin to talk about when his daughter was born premature and had to go to a Columbus (GA) hospital.

Moore   "I went to Columbus to the hospital to be with her. I loved my children for sure."

Moore said he and his wife Brenda would later divorce but how they remained friends and stayed close to raise their children.

Moore   "We were still good friends. She (Brenda) would come over to our house even with my second wife there (Debra). They were good friends too. We (Brenda and Bill) got back together about two months after we divorced. We made a pact we were going to raise those babies. We managed to hold in there…we were divorced longer than we were married."

Moore   "When I was in prison the last time, over there in Jackson for driving without a license, that is when Brenda went her way. I honestly understand why she left. Things just kind of went from there. She came to see me in Jackson and Unadilla (Dooly County prison). My mama told my daddy. I knew where Brenda was at…I knew who she was seeing."

Who Killed Timothy Wayne Coggins?

When they were arrested, law enforcement kept Moore and Gebhardt apart.

Moore   "We couldn't have contact with one another. Frankie knew what was going on. He did. But like I told all these folks, GBI, Sheriff, if I knew anything about all this I would tell them

Melton   "Do you think Frankie killed Timothy Coggins?"

Moore   "Honestly, I do. That boy's got no right to be dragging my name in(to) something like this."

Melton   "Who do you think helped Frankie?"

Moore   "Honestly, I don't know. If I knew anything about it, I'd tell you."

Melton   "I'm going to be a straight shooter with you. You have been in and out of prison a number of times."

Moore and the author would both laugh.

Moore   "Yes sir, I have. The last time I got sentenced was for driving without a license. Everything I have been in jail for is drinking, driving without a license. I lost my license when I was 17 years old. They came to my mother's house and took my license. I was 40 years old before I got it back.

Melton   "Did you ever try and outrun the police (in a car)?"

Moore   "No sir. That was Frankie."

Most of Bill Moore's arrests, as he said, was for drinking, driving violations. One was even for not having a load (on his pulp-wood truck) secure.

Then again, many of Frankie Gebhardt's arrests were for more violent crimes, fighting, beating up women.

Moore   "He (Frankie) was bad about that. If he didn't get his way (with these women) he was going to threaten, beat them up to make himself look good. To look like a bad ass. Yes sir. That's a lot different than drinking and getting your car towed."

Melton   "Would Frankie have killed somebody over dancing with a white girl.

Moore   "Depending on who the girl was at the time. That's stuff I don't know anything about."

Melton   "There was a lot of talk around town that Coggins slept with Brenda. Is this true?

Moore   "No Sir. There ain't no truth to that. I know that for a fact! I knew her. NO SIR (she didn't)!"

Melton   "So that I have no doubt…I'll just ask you again. Do you think Frankie killed that young man?"

Moore   "Honestly I don't (really) know, it's possible. I've seen Frankie get really mad. He and I have had words (from time to time)."

Moore would then go on to relate the time Frankie threw a brick and knocked out his windshield. The time Gebhardt was sneaking up on him (Moore) with an axe (read what happened in Chapter 2, Black Eyes Without a Soul)."

Moore   "All this stuff…trying to whip my ass because I was seeing his sister. Didn't like it because I was with his sister. Frankie would just tell his kin folks what to and not to do…and they would do it! You can't tell your kin folks what to do! Something's wrong. That's just wrong."

Pulp-wooding…Friends…KKK…The Well

Pulp-wooding

Moore would share that he and his wife Brenda would operate a pulp-wood business. But he never cut any wood in Spalding County. When asked if he had ever cut any wood along Minter Road where Coggins body was found Moore replied,

Moore   "No sir. I didn't cut no wood out there. All the wood I ever cut was in Henry County. Henry County didn't mess with me when I went to cut wood (there). That's where me and Brenda cut wood."

Friends

Several of the witnesses from the Gebhardt trial were discussed.

Willard Sanders   Moore, "Yes I know Willard Sanders. Got to know him through Frankie. I know all them Sanders boys."

Christopher Vaughn   Moore, "I know Chris Vaughn."

Melton   "Is he reliable?"

Moore   "No sir, he is not. All this is his doing. If Chris mentioned my name in any situation it's because of what Frankie has built up in his (Vaughn's) mind. It is because he (Frankie) has always put my name in when he wanted bragging rights (to get Bill in trouble). I mean if Frankie known anything about this, I feel sorry for him."

Ruth Elizabeth "Mitzie" Guy-*Allegedly with Frankie night of the murder and left town when he began to beat her up (see Chapter 6 and Timetable).*

Moore   "No sir. Only way she knew me is through Frankie. Personally, no sir. She did not know me."

Sandra Bunn-*Frankie' older sister who takes and took care of him.*

Melton   "She can be an intimidating woman."

Moore   "Yes sir. She can be a bully. Sandra is helping pay for that (the defense). Frankie aint' got no money."

The KKK

Melton   "Was Frankie officially in the KKK?"

Moore   "Not as far as I know."

Melton   "Were you?"

Moore   "No sir. Where that is coming from who knows? Coming from folks who know nothing about it."

<u>The Well</u>

In 2018, right before Gebhardt's trial, a dry well was dug up on what had been Gebhardt's property. The property is still owned by the family (see Chapter 11 and Timetable).

Moore   "Yes sir, I know about that well. I know that over the years when me and Brenda lived there with Frankie's mother (Brenda's mother as well), that we were trying to fill up that well. Filling it up with old trash, old clothes that we didn't wear."

Melton   "When you and Frankie were in jail, they went to scrape the well and found a shoe they found out later belonged to Timothy Coggins the victim. Do you know anything about that?"

Moore   "No sir. I remember wearing those kinds of shoes like that...old black (tennis) shoes."

The shoes that were found at the bottom of the well were size 10 Adidas and were white.

"You have five minutes." Last words last thoughts

"You have five minutes," the prison guard sitting behind the author announced. So many more questions to ask. So much more for Bill Moore to talk about.

But the time had come to an end. These were the rules which are strictly enforced in any Georgia prison facility.

Melton   "Bill. Anything else you want to add before I go?

Moore   "Right now it's kindda got me on edge, If I had anything to do with this? I feel as if I am going crazy (trying to remember). I've just about told you my whole situation. When you get to my age….," *Moore began to cry again. The author could not hand him a Kleenex through the glass as it was against the rules to give a prisoner anything, even a tissue. Both the author and Moore began to laugh at not being able to pass a Kleenex through the barred window.*

Moore   "I remember sending my little brother up there (when Moore and Brenda were dating) to tell Brenda that I loved her," he said shaking his head as if remembering a long time ago and the anger Brenda's brother Frankie had inside. With a faraway look in his eyes, Moore remembered,

Moore   "A lot of things could have been different, I guess. But you can't go back and change (anything)."

When asked about if he thought Frankie would get a new trial and would he, Moore, testify if a new trial took place, Moore replied,

Moore   "I don't look for Frankie to win no new trial. I really don't."

In prison Bill Moore says that he keeps to himself. Perhaps he has learned this in past incarcerations.

Moore   "I want to do my time and get out."

Guard   "Time's up (for the interview)."

Melton   "Yes ma'm."

The author then asked Moore if he could say a prayer with him.

Melton   "I don't know if you are a Christian man or not, but could we say a prayer?"

Moore   "Yes sir. I pray every day."

The prayer asked for forgiveness, for Jesus to save the soul of Bill Moore. To give him a fresh start every day and to help him find peace.

When the prayer ended Moore, again with tears in his eyes, turned to the author and asked,

Moore   "Mr. Quimby. Please tell my little girl Brandy I love her."

Melton   "I'll do that Bill. I will."

Moore   "And you drive safely back."

+++++++

With that Bill Moore returned to his wheelchair and left for his small cell. He is prisoner 591759 sleeping on the bottom bunk of wing D-1, cell 131 of the Johnson State Prison in faraway Wrightsville, GA.

The first time the author saw Bill Moore was at a magistrate hearing held in November 2017. He and Gebhardt had been arrested and were about to be charged with the murder of Timothy Wayne Coggins, a crime committed 34 years prior.

Moore looked repentant and haggard as he sat with his lawyer listening to the changes against him and his onetime friend.

The once haggard Bill Moore now looks healthy, but still full of remorse.

Afterall it's a long time until release and parole.

Did Bill Moore murder Timothy Wayne Coggins? Only the Lord know for sure.

Perhaps now, after all has been said and done, the family of the victim Timothy Wayne Coggins *and* William Franklin Moore can both find peace and understanding.

And yes. I did call Brandy and told her that her father loved her. She cried.

Perhaps the Bible expresses it best for both the Coggins family and William Franklin Moore:

"…and the peace of God, which surpasses all understanding, will guard your hearts and your minds…"
                    Philippians 4:7

                              OQMIII

An Interview with Franklin George Gebhardt ?

Georgia State Prison
Reidsville, GA

Numerous requests have been made by the author asking for an interview with Franklin George Gebhardt, the murderer, incarcerated in the Reidsville, GA state prison. Formal documents have been signed and forwarded to proper authorities. Gebhardt's sister, Sandra Bunn, has been supportive of the author's interview requests. But to date (September 17, 2019), no permission has been given nor calls placed to Gebhardt's attorney, Larkin Lee returned.

If the author does receive permission to interview Gebhardt, he will head to Reidsville and get Frankie's side of the story. An update will be published if this happens.

But for the time being, in Reidsville, GA, 177 miles southeast of Griffin and Sunnyside, Franklin George Gebhardt sits in his prison cell day…after day…after day.

My thoughts

I have been interested in this case most recently for about two years. When I first went to the magistrate hearing at the end of November 2017 until now, a two-year time period has come and gone. But, in reality, it has been something I have found unsettling for 36 years.

In 1983 I was publisher of the Griffin Daily News. I vividly remember when we got the call from law enforcement and reporter Carl Elmore went to the crime scene in October 1983. Really it was only yesterday.

What I have wondered and pondered these many years is why…why was a young black man brutally and savagely killed in the outposts of Spalding County? But then again why does anyone murder another human being? I remember the grief-stricken family both at the time and at the June 2018 trial. I remember how our reporting hit a wall of no information…a wall that would be unscalable until new evidence was presented, and a relentless sheriff and prosecutor would head to trial.

During the months of November 2017 to June 2018, new evidence seemed to come forth almost every day. This was astounding to have a cold murder case move forward after 34 years. The percentage of a cold case coming to trial is small…after 34 years nearly zero. With evidence lost, less than stellar witnesses appearing in the courtroom, and an overall sense of wondering the proverbial who, what, when, where, why and how, this reporter never felt a guilty verdict would come back from the jury. The murder had simply happened too long ago.

But **GUILTY** did come back against Franklin George Gebhardt that sultry June afternoon. Five counts of guilty would send the man, who had been in and out of the Georgia penal system for most of his life, to Reidsville for the rest of his life.

Lady Justice, with her infinite knowledge of right and wrong, would win that summer afternoon in our Spalding County Georgia courtroom in 2018.

It has been an amazing personal journey for the author of this book to interview the numerous sources; both those who did not mind going, "on the record," and those who were fearful of having their name(s) in print. Do I believe the sources I interviewed both free and behind bars? Yes. To the person I believe they were telling the truth. I am not naïve, just been around long enough to tell the spoken truth or not.

In 1983 our racial relations in Griffin and Spalding County were improving. While not as good as today, we were a more open-minded community than many. Conditions and understanding simply had to be corrected. The wrongs had to be made right.

While 1983 was decades away from the 1960's, the brutal and savage killing still horrified our community.

Do I think Franklin George Gebhardt had a part in the murder of Timothy Wayne Coggins?

I do.

I think Frankie was in such a rage with the thought of a black man dancing with, boyfriend of, perhaps sleeping with a white woman, that he sought Coggins out and methodically killed him that October night.

Did Frankie think it was perhaps his baby sister Brenda Coggins had slept with?

I believe Frankie thought it might be Brenda, but I also believe it was not her.

Evidence shows that clothing, a chain, knives, were found in the dried-out water well next to the home Frankie lived in. Was this evidence really his? Did he throw the items down the well?

I believe he did in the belief that the items would never be found.

Was it a miracle or luck that these items were found in the well…discovered by a new way to drill for evidence called hydrovac?

I would call it the intervention of a higher power that day.

Do I think Frankie was assisted in his crime of passion?

I do. I believe Ruth Elizabeth "Mitzie" Guy knew about the murder maybe even watched him as he killed the young man. But Mitzie Guy is dead. We will never know.

I also believe another person, a man, helped with the murder. Was this Bill Moore?

I don't believe it was Moore.

In the interview this reporter conducted with Moore at the Johnson State Prison, I believe the truth came out. Moore did not have a trial. He was scared he too would get life in prison. Thus, he pled guilty. Twenty years is a long time to be incarcerated, but Bill knew the verdict Frankie had received and he was almost certainly to receive the same.

Bill Moore has done some terrible and stupid things in his life. He has been in and out of prison more times than you can count on your fingers and toes. But I do not believe murder is one of them.

The old saying is, "there are no guilty men (women) in prison." But Moore's statement to me about Frankie throwing his name in and out of situations is solid. I also believe that Frankie was jealous, very jealous when Bill began dating his baby sister, Brenda. You see Bill had wheels. He could go places. His compadre Frankie was now playing second fiddle when Brenda came into the picture.

That said, do I believe that someone is still walking around that may been a party to killing Coggins?

I do. Whether they are still alive or have died with that secret, no one will ever know.

Now as for Frankie.

I believe that, as hard as it is to believe, after all these years I truly believe Frankie does not remember killing Timothy Wayne Coggins. *I truly believe this.*

With all the drugs, alcohol, and good time thunder Frankie consumed, his brain may have forgotten this atrocious incident. It would be impossible for most folks to forget a murder they had committed. But look at Gebhardt's arrest and criminal record. He has been in and out of prison for assault, battery, vicious and violent crimes. He knows the Georgia penal system very well. Is

he a man who is quick to anger and become enraged?
YES…definitely yes.

Frankie Gebhardt had his way in and around Sunnyside for years. He began to think he was above the law. And he was until Sheriff Dix, GBI agent Coleman and prosecutors Coker and Broder discovered the new evidence.

When he was arrested for sexual battery and was in prison, Sheriff Darrell Dix began his elected term of office. People called and gave Dix the tips he needed to make the arrest. These same people had been scared to talk when Frankie was out of jail. Even though he may have by now seemed to be a harmless old man who lived simply with his animals, Gebhardt was still in the eyes of many that same bully, thug, and killer.

Gebhardt had bullied his last. The new lawmen and women of Griffin and Spalding County did not fear Frankie's wrath. It was long time, but justice was served.

I have been impressed by the unwavering faith of the Coggins family that justice would one day be served. That the ruthless murder of their brother, their son, their uncle, their nephew, their cousin would not be in vain. The family nor the community gave up on this quest. That June 2018 afternoon in the Spalding County Courthouse, those many years of frustration, turned into fulfillment, a promise to Timothy Wayne Coggins. The many years of prayers were answered.

Most of all I admire, appreciate and love our community of Griffin and Spalding County. This is a community that has always wanted the best for itself and its citizens. Our law enforcement and prosecutors protect our citizens. We as a community came together and began to get over the prejudice that have lingered for so long in this area we love as the South.

It was indeed a new day when the verdict was read and the killer(s) led from the courtroom, never to taste freedom again.

Justice is sweet, especially after 34 long years.

But one thing I kept hearing in the back of my mind as I put these words to paper…

This indeed was a victory for goodness and justice. The darkness was swept away by the light of righteousness.

Is this book perfect grammatically and punctuations exactly where they should be?

No.

Are there spelling errors?

Hopefully not but I bet there are.

Have I gotten the past, present and future tenses correct within my sentence structure?

Bet there are plenty of errors here.

But…what this book is…it is an accurate and honest effort by the author to report the truth of this senseless and horrific tragedy…100%.

The one thing that I ask is that the reader remember the main message of this book.

Remember…in the end…the Good shall win out over evil, each and every time.

Thank you for taking your time to read this book.

OQMIII

Franklin George Gebhardt-Rap Sheet

Gebhardt used numerous names on his arrest records.

Here are but a few:

KNOWN ALIASES

A.K.A. GEBHARDT,FRAMKLIN GEORGE
A.K.A. GEBHARDT,FRANK GEORGE
A.K.A. GEBHARDT,FRANKIE
A.K.A. GEBHARDT,FRANKIE G
A.K.A. GEBHARDT,FRANKIE GEORGE
A.K.A. GEBHARDT,FRANKLIN G
A.K.A. GEBHARDT,FRANKLIN GEORGE
A.K.A. GEBHARDT,FRANKLYN GEORGE
A.K.A. GEBHART,FRANKIE GEORGE
A.K.A. GEBHART,FRANKLAND GEORGE
A.K.A. GEGHARDT,FRANKLIN GEORGE

FBI Number   89745R4
State ID Number   GA00535577
Georgia Diagnostic Center ID 0000039998

White
Male
5ft 6inches tall
270 pounds

DOB 08/19/1958 or 08/19/1959 (1960)
Used different birthdates
SS XXX-XX-XXXX

Drivers License XXXXXXXXXX

1704 Patterson Road
Griffin, GA 30223

Arrests
_____

1. 01/29/1983-Henry Co SO -Criminal Damage
    2nd Degree

Disposition-Guilty-Convicted-Adjudicated
11/09/1984-Felony
Jail Term Began 11/09/1984 Admitted
12/03/1984 Released 03/14/1985

2. **97-SR-4088**
   06/25/1997 Offense Date
   Filed 07/23/1997

3. State of Georgia vs Frankie Gebhardt
   Public Drunkenness
   Misdemeanor
   State Court-Judge Sid Esary
   Cash Bond $103 fine and add ons 08/21/1997

4. **97R-767**
   Date of offense 07-07-1997
   Felony
   Filed on 10/07/1997
   Aggravated Assault
   State of Georgia vs Frankie Gebhardt
   Superior Court
   Johnny Mostiler Attorney
   Opened 10/07/1997
   11/13/1997
   Guilty Verdict CSCD Time 1st year intensive probation
   stay away from victim Deborah Pruett and pay
   $2925 fines and fees

   12-23-1997 Waiver of Hearing and Consent Order
   to Revoke Probation Gebhardt to enter and complete
   the GRIPP counseling
   6-8-98 Waiver of Hearing and consent order revoking
   probation
   6-25-98 Order to continue probation supervision
   5-27-99 Waiver of Hearing and consent order

modifying probation
9-8-99 Waiver of hearing and consent order
revoking probation
3-28-2001 Waiver of Hearing and consent order modifying
probation
6-17-2002 Petition for modification/revocation of probation
Hearing June 28, 2002 Judge Edwards

8-16-2002
Waiver of Right to Counsel
Waiver of hearing and consent order revoking probation
Revoke Balance of 2 months and 29 days to Spalding
County Jail. Credit for time served since 04-20-2002

07/07/1997 SCSO Aggravated Assault
Disposition-Guilty-Convicted-Adjudicated
11/13/1997-Felony
$2925 Fine Probation for 5 years

5. **99SR-5073**
    Offense 05-13-1999
    Filed 06/04/1999
    Misdemeanor Judge Sid Esary
    Public Drunkeness
    07/27/1999
    Guilty Fine of $103 and fees

6. **02SR-3658** State of GA vs
    Franklin George Gebphardt
    Offense date 03/22/2002
    Driving while unlicensed
    05/28/2002   Suspended license
    6 months and $315.50 fines plus fees
    Judge Esary

7. **02SR-8517**   State of Georgia vs
Franklin George Gebhardt
Simple Battery 04/20-2002 offense date
Judge Esary....time served NOT to be around
Tammy McCulley
7/30/20002

8. 01/17/2003 Civil Suit Filed
By Sister Sandra Bunn #03D0211
03/D-0211
Civil Suit by Sister Sandra Ruth Gebhardt
01/17/2003
Settled 01-29/2003

03-D-0211
Filed 01-17-2003

Dispossessory **EVICITION**
Sandra Bunn vs Franklin Gebphadt
Default Judgement 1/29/2003
Ann A Gregory Magistrate Court
Ruled in favor of Bunn...Plaintiff

9. **99V-316**
GA Dept of Human Resources,
Franklin C. Gebhardt vs Franklin G. Gebhardt
2-22-1999 Child Support Recovery
03-26-1999 Case dismissed Judge Edwards

10. **99V-1332**
GA Dept of Human Resources,
Franklin C. Gebhardt vs Franklin G. Gebhardt
08-05-1999 Petition for Contempt
10-29-1999 Contempt Judge Edwards
11-9-1999 Conversion Judgement

11. **03R-512**
05/05/2003-SCSO-Aggravated Assault

5/20/2003 Motion for Bond
5/30/2003 Bond Denied
6-6-2003 Special Conditions…intensive probation
4-23-2004 Revoke probation
7-23-2008 FIFA $1250 plus $138 court costs
Disposition-Guilty-Convicted-Adjudicated 06/06/2003-
Felony
$125 Fine   Probation 5 years   Restitution

12. **04V-139**
GA Dept of Human Resources,
Franklin C. Gebhardt vs Franklin G. Gebhardt
08-06-2004 Contempt Judge Johnnie L. Caldwell
09/20/2005 Notice of Hearing
10/12/2005 Conversion Judgement
02/24-2006 Contempt
02/28-2006 Order of Contempt

13. **08SR-5131** The State of Georgia vs
Franklin George Gebhardt
Disorderly Conduct 08/04/2008
09/23/2008   Guilty Judge Esary
$340.50 fine plus fees
Probation   Misdemeanor

14. **09V2927**

GA Dept of Human Resources,
Franklin C. Gebhardt vs Franklin G. Gebhardt
12/10/2009 Conversion Docket-Petition for Contempt
02/25/2010 Conversion Judgement
Judge Chris Edwards

15. **11R-602** Aggravated Assault   Battery
5-18-11 Offense Date
Filed 10/3/2011
Superior Court-Judge Sams
2-6-12 Disposition Nolle Prosequi

The State will not be able to Prove this case
beyond a reasonable Doubt
George H. Weldon attorney
Bonded by Sandra Bunn

16. **11V-985**
GA Dept of Human Resources,
Franklin C. Gebhardt vs Franklin G. Gebhardt
06-03-2011 Again Contempt
09/20/2011 Again Conversion Judgement
Judge Edwards

17. **12V-1860**
GA Dept of Human Resources,
Franklin C. Gebhardt vs Franklin G. Gebhardt
11/26/12 Again Comtempt
01/09/13 Again Conversion Judgement Judge Edwards

18. **13SR-221** State of GA vs Franklin George Gebhardt
1/15/2013 Driving while license suspended
              Failure to maintain lane
2/26/2013 $708 fine plus $39 a month probation

19. **17R-155**   7/2/15 False Imprisonment
Sexual Battery and Battery Sex Crimes
State of GA vs Franklin George Gebhardt
again charged 9/3/2016
False Imprisonment was Felony
  Sexual Battery was a Misdemeanor
  Filed in court 4-28-17
  Charles William Lamar Bunn posted bond

July 12, 2017 Harry Charles filed a motion to have a
MENTAL EVALUATION on Gebhardt
Charles is a public defender and attorney for
7/17/2017 LARKIN LEE FILED AS ATTORNEY
Notice of Trial 8/28/2017
10/6/2017 Plea and Confinement
 False Imprisonment plea was Nol Pros (NP)

4 charges of Sexual battery was found guilty
12 months to serve

20. 10/13/2017-SCSO & GBI
    17-FAH 1990   Coggins Original Case
    18-R-105A Superior Ct.

5 Charges
1) Malice Murder
2) Felony Murder
3) Aggravated Assault
4) Aggravated Battery
5) Concealing the Death of Another

Tuesday, June 26, 2018
Found Guilty on all five charges
Life in Prison plus 30 years-probation to run concurrently

Misdemeanor and Felony Charges against Gebhardt
These are charges and indictments that have resulted in which Gebhardt was found guilty, and/or not guilty, and/or Nolle Prosequi by the defense (Alphabetical order).

1. Aggravated Assault-05-18-2011
2. Aggravated Assault-*Coggins Case*
3. Aggravated Battery-*Coggins Case*
4. Bail-Failure to Appear After Release for a Misdemeanor
5. Battery
6. Battery-Sex Crimes
7. Child Support Recovery
8. Civil Suit-Eviction
9. Concealing Death of Another -*Coggins Case*
10. Contempt
11. Disregarding Traffic Control Device
12. Disorderly Conduct
13. Driving while License Suspended or Revoked
14. Driving without a License
15. Drugs-Trafficking in Meth or Cocaine Base
16. Failure to Maintain Lane-Driving

17. Failure to Appear
18. False Imprisonment
19. Felony Murder-*Coggins Case*
20. Fugitive in State
21. Lack of Use of Safety Belts
22. Malice Murder-*Coggins Case*
23. Possession of Firearm/Knife During
        Commission Commit Certain Felony
24. Probation Violation
25. Public Drunkenness
26. Revoke Probation
27. Sexual Battery
28. Shoplifting-Theft
29. Simple Battery
30. Speeding
31. Theft by Receiving Stolen Property Felony #1
32. Theft by Receiving Stolen Property Felony #2
33. Theft by Receiving Stolen Property Felony #3

Fugitive in State | Driving While License Suspended
or Revoked-Failure to Maintain Insurance | Traffic / Driving
Without a License - 1st Offense 2191 | Drugs / Trafficking
in Meth. or Cocaine Base - 10 G or More, But Less Than 28 G
-
1st Offense 881 | Bail / Failure to Appear After Release
for a Misdemeanor (Not Used From 6/98 to 6/08) 367
Use of Safety Belts in Passenger Vehicles | Failure to Appear
Theft by Shoplifting - Misdemeanor | Probation Violation
(When
Probation Terms Are Altered) | Probation Violation-
Disregarding Traffic Control Device | Driving While
License Suspended or Revoked (Misdemeanor)-
Possession of Firearm or Knife During Commission of
or Attempt to Commit Certain Felonies | Theft by Receiving
Stolen Property - Felony | Speeding | Theft by Receiving
Stolen Property - Felony#2 Theft by Receiving Stolen Property
Felony#3 Driving While License Suspended or Revoked
(Misdemeanor)

William Franklin Moore, Sr.-Rap Sheet

Moore used numerous names on his arrest records. Here are but a few:

KNOWN ALIASES

A.K.A. MOORE,BILL
A.K.A. MOORE,BO
A.K.A. MOORE,WILLIAM F
A.K.A. MOORE,WILLIAM FRANK
A.K.A. MOORE,WILLIAM FRANKLIN
A.K.A. MOORE,WILLIAM FRANKLIN S
A.K.A. MOORE,WILLIE FRANK

FBI Number   981031R8
State ID Number 00579875

Georgia Diagnostic Center (Jail) Number
0000591750

White
Male
Height 5 feet 11 inches tall
Weight 270 pounds

DOB 05/06/1959
Drivers License XXXXXXXX
SS XXX-XX-XXXX

Residences
-105 S 11th St
-1466 Kilgore Road B-3
-41-A Carey's MHP 1996
-1561 Patterson Road
-28 Ramsey Circle
all Griffin, GA 30223

Arrests
_____

1. 12/31/1978 Lamar County
DUI-Theft by Taking-Probation Violation
Habitual Violator-Probation

2. 05/05/1978-DUI

3. 07/25/1980   GBI and SCSO
   Criminal Interference with Govt. Prop
$1550 fine 2 years probation -Spalding 00579875

4. 09/01/1994-DUI

5. 03/11/1996-Lamar County
   DUI
   Habitual Violator
   Criminal Interference with Govt. Prop.
   Probation Violation
   Theft by Taking

6. 01/27/1995-Lamar County
   and Monroe County SO
   DUI
   Habitual Violator
   Criminal Interference with Govt. Prop.
   Probation Violation
   Theft by Taking

7. **96SR-4484**
   06/25/1996
   Public Drunkenness
   Trial 08-15-1996   Judge Esary
   Appears to be a bond forfeiture

8. 03/24/1997-Lamar and Henry SO
   DUI **97-CR-0166**
   Habitual Violator
   Criminal Interference with Govt. Prop.
   Probation Violation
   Theft by Taking
   Restitution $750 Fees 5 yrs Probation
   Revoke CC to time now serving
   Sentence Confine 3 years Probation
   Began April 1997   Ended Sept 1998

9. **00-COV-118**
   Littering on Public Property 7-28-2000
   fine 8-9-2000   Judge Cavanaugh $393
   plus clean up service

10. **01-COV-049**
    5-24-01 County Ordinance Violation
    Failure to Secure Load
    6-20-01 Judge Cavanaugh $263

11. **02SR-4592**
    08/25-2001 Date of Offense
    Failure to have Insurance 4-15-2002
    Violation of Limited Permit 4-15-2002
    Bench Warrant   5-28-2002
    02-04-2003
    $312.50 plus 34.25…plus $39 month probation
    fees…court fees
    Probation

12. **02SR-13144**
    Bench Warrant 12-16-02
    Failure to Appear   Judge Esary
    11-13-2002 No Brake Lights
    5-13-2003 Cash Bond Forfeiture

$71.75 plus 62.50

13. **03SR-2167**
Offense Date 04/20/2002
Disorderly Conduct
Obstruction of an officer
Court Case 06/03/2003
Fine $128 plus fees
Probation 39.00 a month

14. **Lamar County Clerk**
2C-152   10/08/2002
Karen Martin attorney
09/10/2002   Incident
01/09/2003 Pre Trial Hearing
-Terrorist Threats
-Criminal Trespass
-Disorderly Conduct
-Public Drunk

15. **03-SR-3811**
DUI, Speeding 72 in a 55 zone,
Violation of an open container
09/03/2002
Probation 03/30/2005
FIFA Issued 10/20/2005

16. 01/13/2009   Henry County-DUI

17. **11S-1284**
11/02/2011   Spalding County
First Financial vs Wm. Moore
Wife Debra   apparently forfeited $456.55
02/08/2012   Spalding County-Judgement $564.55

18. 03/05/2013-Terroristic Threat 03/13/13 Felony-GA

19. 04/09/2014-Georgia-Possession of Cocaine

20. 05/29/2014-Georgia-Bench Warrant-Speeding

21. 06/15/2014-Georgia-Following too Closely
    Aggressive Driving

22. 08/16/18   SCSO & GBI   **18-R-105B** Superior Ct.

5 Charges
1) Malice Murder
2) Felony Murder
3) Aggravated Assault
4) Aggravated Battery
5) Concealing the Death of Another

Tuesday, August 16, 2018
Plead Guilty to Voluntary Manslaughter
and Concealing the Death of Another
Sentenced to 20 years in prison plus
10 years-probation to begin when out of prison

Also at one time ESCAPE...maybe from Probation
(See below Butts County 07-03-1991)

Misdemeanor and Felony Charges against Moore
These are charges and indictments that have resulted in which Moore
was found guilty and/or not guilty (Alphabetical Order).

1. Aggravated Assault-*Coggins Case*
2. Aggravated Battery-*Coggins Case*
3. Aggressive Driving
4. Bench Warrant-Speeding
5. Concealing Death of Another-*Coggins Case*
6. Criminal Interference with Government Property
7. Criminal Tresspass
8. Disorderly Conduct

9. DUI-Driving while under the Influence
10. Escape
11. Failure to have Insurance
12. Failure to Appear in Court
13. Felony Murder-*Coggins Case*
14. Following too Closely
15. Habitual Violator
16. Habitual Violations-Driving
17. Habitual Violator-NPOI
18. Littering on Public Property
19. Malice Murder-C*oggins Case*
20. No Brake Lights
21. Obstruction of an Officer
22. Other Misdemeanor
23. Possession of Cocaine-Felony
24. Probation Violation-Felony
25. Public Drunk
26. Public Drunkenness
27. Speeding
28. Terroristic Threats and Acts-Felony
29. Theft by Taking
30. Violation-County Ordinance-Failure to Secure Load
31. Violation of a Limited Permit
32. Violation of an Open Container

Driving Habtl Violator | Other Misdemeanor | Escape-Habitual Violator - Npoi | Driving Under The Influence (Driving While Under The Influence) | Habitual Violator-Probation Violation - Fel | Theft by Taking | Criminal Interference with Gov Property | Terroristic Threats and Acts (Felony) | Possession of Cocaine (Felony)
Bench Warrant - Speeding (Specified Speed)
Following Too Closely (Misdemeanor)
Aggressive Driving (Misdemeanor)

Christopher Joseph Vaughn
Rap Sheet

Vaughn used numerous names on his
arrest records. Here are but a few:

KNOWN ALIASES

A.K.A. VAUGHN,CHRIS JOSEPH
A.K.A. VAUGHN,CHRISTOPHER
A.K.A. VAUGHN,CHRISTOPHER J
A.K.A. VAUGHN,CHRISTOPHER JOSEP
A.K.A. VAUGHT,CHRISTOPHER JOSEP
A.K.A. VAUSHN,CHRISTOPHER JOSEP

DOB August 22, 1973

GDC ID: 0000786186
STATE OF GEORGIA -
CURRENT SENTENCES

    1. CASE NO: 599314

OFFENSE: CHILD MOLESTATION
CONVICTION COUNTY: SPALDING COUNTY
CRIME COMMIT DATE: 06/21/2004
SENTENCE LENGTH: 10 YEARS, 0 MONTHS, 0 DAYS

    2. CASE NO: 599314

OFFENSE: CHILD MOLESTATION
CONVICTION COUNTY: SPALDING COUNTY
CRIME COMMIT DATE: 06/21/2004
SENTENCE LENGTH: 10 YEARS, 0 MONTHS, 0 DAYS

    3. CASE NO: 599314

OFFENSE: SEX EXPLOITATION CHILD
CONVICTION COUNTY: SPALDING COUNTY
CRIME COMMIT DATE: 06/21/2004
SENTENCE LENGTH: 10 YEARS, 0 MONTHS, 0 DAYS

4. CASE NO: 599314

OFFENSE: CHILD MOLESTATION
CONVICTION COUNTY: SPALDING COUNTY
CRIME COMMIT DATE: 06/16/2004
SENTENCE LENGTH: 20 YEARS, 0 MONTHS, 0 DAYS

5. CASE NO: 599314

OFFENSE: SEX EXPLOITATION CHILD
CONVICTION COUNTY: SPALDING COUNTY
CRIME COMMIT DATE: 06/16/2004
SENTENCE LENGTH: 10 YEARS, 0 MONTHS, 0 DAYS

6. CASE NO: 599314

OFFENSE: SEX EXPLOITATION CHILD
CONVICTION COUNTY: SPALDING COUNTY
CRIME COMMIT DATE: 06/16/2004
SENTENCE LENGTH: 10 YEARS, 0 MONTHS, 0 DAYS

7. CASE NO: 599314

OFFENSE: CHILD MOLESTATION
CONVICTION COUNTY: SPALDING COUNTY
CRIME COMMIT DATE: 04/01/2004
SENTENCE LENGTH: 20 YEARS, 0 MONTHS, 0 DAYS

STATE OF GEORGIA - PRIOR SENTENCES

8. CASE NO: 403558

OFFENSE: THEFT BY DECEPTION
CONVICTION COUNTY: SPALDING COUNTY
CRIME COMMIT DATE: 11/12/2001
SENTENCE LENGTH: 2 YEARS, 0 MONTHS, 0 DAYS

9. CASE NO: 403558

OFFENSE: theft by taking
CONVICTION COUNTY: COWETA COUNTY
CRIME COMMIT DATE: 05/31/1999
SENTENCE LENGTH: 0 YEARS, 12 MONTHS, 0 DAYS

10. CASE NO: 403558

OFFENSE: ENTERING VEHICLE
CONVICTION COUNTY: COWETA COUNTY
CRIME COMMIT DATE: 05/31/1999
SENTENCE LENGTH: 1 YEARS, 0 MONTHS, 0 DAYS

11. CASE NO: 403558

OFFENSE: FORG 1ST BEF 7/1/12
CONVICTION COUNTY: SPALDING COUNTY
CRIME COMMIT DATE: 06/23/1998
SENTENCE LENGTH: 4 YEARS, 0 MONTHS, 0 DAYS

12. CASE NO: 403558

OFFENSE: FORG 1ST BEF 7/1/12
CONVICTION COUNTY: SPALDING COUNTY
CRIME COMMIT DATE: 06/23/1998
SENTENCE LENGTH: 4 YEARS, 0 MONTHS, 0 DAYS

13. CASE NO: 403558

OFFENSE: FORG 1ST BEF 7/1/12
CONVICTION COUNTY: SPALDING COUNTY
CRIME COMMIT DATE: 06/23/1998
SENTENCE LENGTH: 4 YEARS, 0 MONTHS, 0 DAYS

14. CASE NO: 403558

OFFENSE: FORG 1ST BEF 7/1/12
CONVICTION COUNTY: SPALDING COUNTY
CRIME COMMIT DATE: 06/23/1998
SENTENCE LENGTH: 4 YEARS, 0 MONTHS, 0 DAYS

15. CASE NO: 403558

OFFENSE: FORG 1ST BEF 7/1/12
CONVICTION COUNTY: SPALDING COUNTY
CRIME COMMIT DATE: 06/23/1998
SENTENCE LENGTH: 4 YEARS, 0 MONTHS, 0 DAYS

16. CASE NO: 403558

OFFENSE: THEFT BY TAKING
CONVICTION COUNTY: SPALDING COUNTY
CRIME COMMIT DATE: N/A
SENTENCE LENGTH: 0 YEARS, 60 MONTHS, 0 DAYS

17. CASE NO: 403558

OFFENSE: THEFT BY TAKING
CONVICTION COUNTY: SPALDING COUNTY

CRIME COMMIT DATE: N/A
SENTENCE LENGTH: 0 YEARS, 60 MONTHS, 0 DAYS

18. CASE NO: 403558

OFFENSE: FORG 1ST BEF 7/1/12
CONVICTION COUNTY: FAYETTE COUNTY
CRIME COMMIT DATE: N/A
SENTENCE LENGTH: 8 YEARS, 0 MONTHS, 0 DAYS

STATE OF GEORGIA - INCARCERATION HISTORY

INCARCERATION BEGIN: 03/27/2006

INCARCERATION END: ACTIVE

INCARCERATION BEGIN: 04/04/2002

INCARCERATION END: 01/31/2004

INCARCERATION BEGIN: 12/15/1999

INCARCERATION END: 08/28/2001

INCARCERATION BEGIN: 11/24/1998

INCARCERATION END: 04/11/1999

Theft by Taking - Fel | Return for Court-
Parole Violation | Entering Auto | Forgery-
1st Degree | Sexual Exploitation of Children - 3cts
Theft by Taking - MV | Child Molestation - 3cts | Forgery-
1st Degree - 2cts | Child Molestation - 2cts | Theft by
Deception | Entering Vehicle | Probation Violation-
Forgery 1st Degree | Child Molestation | Sexual Battery-
Criminal Trespass | Probation Violation - Orig: Financial
Identity Fraud

Timeline

December 31, 1978
First recorded arrest for William Franklin Moore
DUI, Theft by taking, Probation Violation
Habitual Violator-Lamar County

January 29, 1983
First Recorded arrest for Franklin George Gebhardt
Henry County Sheriff's Office
Criminal Damage Second Degree
Felony-Jail December 1984-March 1985

Friday, October 7, 1983
Timothy Wayne Coggins last seen at People's Choice nightclub leaving with two white men and a white woman. Coggins seen at Carey's MHP with Gebhardt, another white man and Ruth Guy. Gebhardt and Coggins seen arguing by 10-year-old boy, Christopher Joseph Vaughn

Saturday, Sunday, October 8-9, 1983
Coggins killed (estimated time late Saturday PM or early Sunday AM)

Sunday, October 9, 1983
Body found by hunters in woods off Minter Road near Sunnyside, approximately 10 AM

Sunday, October 9, 1983
Investigators called to scene by one of hunters

Monday, October 10, 1983
Report of the murder in the Griffin Daily News

Tuesday, October 12, 1983
Body of Timothy Wayne Coggins identified

Thursday, October 13, 1983
Obituary notice in Griffin Daily News

Friday, October 14, 1983
Coggins funeral at Fuller Chapel UMC, Zebulon

Late October 1983
Gebhardt and Moore suspects in the murder. Alleged to have been in area pulp-wooding where murder occurred. Questioned but later released

Early November 1983
Spalding County Sheriff's Office and GBI exhaust all leads in murder case. Moved on to other cases and investigations

Late 1983-Early 1984
Christopher Joseph Vaughn, approximately 10-years-old, overheard with others, Gebhardt brag about the murder at a party.

1988
Information came forward in case-Gebhardt and Moore remained suspects but never were charged

1989-2004(05)
Murder investigation all but stopped-Key evidence lost

June 2004
Christopher Joseph Vaughn found guilty of Child Molestation-Sentenced to 50-year prison sentence

2005-07
Christopher Joseph Vaughn began to talk to law
enforcement about murder. Moore and Gebhardt
remained suspects but again were not charged.

2015
GBI Special Agent Jared Coleman assigned to case.
Valid leads began to be found

November 2016
Ben Coker elected Spalding County District Attorney
Darrell Dix elected Spalding County Sheriff

April 2017
Franklin George Gebhardt arrested and jailed
in Spalding County for sexual assault. Was in jail
when arrested for murder in October 2017

Friday, October 13, 2017
Gebhardt and Moore arrested for the murder of
Timothy Wayne Coggins. Sandra Bunn, Lamar Bunn
and Gregory Huffman arrested for obstruction of justice.

Saturday-Sunday, October 14 15, 2017
Bunn-Bunn-Huffman released on bond

Wednesday, November 1, 2017
Bond hearing-Bond denied for both Gebhardt and Moore.
Gebhardt attorney David Studdard
Moore attorney Kevin Hurt
Friday, November 3, 2017
Virgil Brown and Associates became attorneys of record
for

Gebhardt. Harry Charles appointed State of Georgia
Public Defender

Thursday, November 30, 2017
Hearing-Magistrate Court-Rita Cavanaugh Judge
Determined enough evidence to turn over to
Spalding County Grand Jury

Tuesday, December 5, 2017
Spalding County Grand Jury met-Found enough
evidence to take both Gebhardt and Moore to trial. True
Bill. Charged with murder. Case number 17-R-524 A&B

Tuesday, December 5, 2017
Spalding County District Attorney Ben Coker issues
indictments against Gebhardt and Moore

Thursday, Dec. 28, 2017
Plea (unsuccessful) to prevent prosecution of counts
barred by statute of limitations

Sunday, December 31, 2017
Permanent memorial marker on gravesite of Timothy
Wayne Coggins at Faith Chapel United Methodist
Church. Family now could rest believing monument
would not be desecrated by vandals. Coggins finally
laid to rest.

Thurs., January 11, 2018
Gebhardt and Moore waived arraignment

Tuesday, January 16, 2018
Request to quash indictment (unsuccessful)

Tuesday, January 16, 2018
Request for mental evaluation for Gebhardt

Tuesday, January 16, 2018
Witness List filed with court

Thursday, January 25, 2018
Arraignment for Gebhardt and Moore

Thursday, January 25, 2018
Motion by Gebhardt to change venue and move trial to another town due to inflammatory and prejudicial pre-trial publicity

Thursday, February 8, 2018
Gebhardt's attorney requested separate trial from Moore (sever the trial)

Motion by Gebhardt's attorney for DA to reveal any type of deal, promises or grants of immunity to another

Gebhardt's attorney requested private access to client

Request by Gebhardt's attorney to test evidence documents
1) Hair Collected by GBI
2) Homemade club fashioned from a chair or table leg recovered from crime scene
3) Clothing recovered from victim's body
4) Blood stained dollar bill passed at the EZ Shop and recovered by the SCSO

Monday, March 19, 2018
Motions to be presented before Judge Sams. Motions hearings postponed due to fact mental evaluation on Gebhardt had not been returned by the state. Hearing

postponed until Thursday, March 22, 2018

Monday, March 19, 2018
Spalding County Grand Jury. Transferred all the charges
to clean up dates. New case number 18-R-105 A&B

Thursday, March 22, 2018
Motions hearing continued. Judge Sams and Gebhardt's
attorney Scott Johnston went to Judge's chambers and
returned. Judge Sams shared with court that report from
Gebhardt mental evaluation was he was mentally
stable to stand trial. File was SEALED by court on
May 29, 2018.

Other motions approved that day:
1. Gebhardt and Moore would not be tried together but
separately. This is called severing the trial. Now
Gebhardt would be assigned case number 18-R-105 A
and Moore would be assigned court case 18-R-105B

2. Motion for Spalding County District Attorney to provide
all information to defense was mutually approved by
prosecution and defense

3. No "deals" had been made with any witness by
the District Attorney's office. If any were made the
defense would be aware of it

4. No hearsay evidence would be introduced (Ruth Guy
and Casey Moore who were now deceased)
*RUTH GUY...made two statements to law enforcement
in 1983. Said Gebhardt was with her October 7, 1983.
At 11:15 p.m. left with Moore to take him home. Gebhardt
then returned and spent night. Guy had filed domestic*

violence against Geb on October 21 and 24, 1983.
Shortly after that left state for good…never to return.
Casey Moore said he was with Geb. Thursday, October
6, and Saturday, October 8, 1983. Geb. Was doing work
for him.

5. All notes by defense and District Attorney would be available if requested by either side. It was noted that Sheriff Dix's notes would also be shared

6. Judge Sams took under advisement a motion by Gebhardt's attorneys that a change of venue be approved due to prior publicity in the case, particularly with the Atlanta Journal and Constitution newspaper and the CNN News Network.

Wed. April 11, 2018
GBI Agent Jared Coleman met
with Judge Scott Ballard in Fayette County office and obtained search warrant:
1) To excavate the well at 1704 Patterson Road property with Atlanta HydroVac. This is an alternative to digging since there was concern about the structure of the house that was nearby if digging began (law enforcement had considered excavation May 10, 2017 but due to structure weakness and traditional drilling methods, did not proceed.

Thurs. April 12, 2018
Well on Gebhardt property drilled.

Friday, April 13, 2018
Articles found by the water excavation included knife handle and blade, clothing, trash, shoes, part of a chair,

rope, spoon, auto parts and trash. Appeared that trash had been within well and burned.

Thurs. April 27, 2018
Christopher Joseph Vaughn entered into cell with Frankie Gebhardt wired to record their conversation. Law enforcement hoped that Gebhardt would admit to the murder. He did not.

Friday, April 28, 2018
Hearing scheduled but postponed

Friday, May 18, 2018
Hearing for motions in Gebhardt case (Moore severed from case and will have another trial).

1. Notice to proceed with the evidence
2. Defense asked statements by Vaughn be suppressed
3. Defense asked statements by Patrick Douglas be suppressed. Said most would be hearsay
4. Defense asked that search warrants not be permitted
5. Judge Sams turned down request from defense for all motions Vaughn, Douglas and search warrants

Gebhardt Trial

Monday, June 18, 2018
Trial 18-R105-A State of Georgia vs Franklin George Gebhardt begins

Tuesday, June 19, 2018
Jury selected and charged for Gebhardt trial

Wed-Mon-June 20-25, 2018
Prosecution presents witnesses

Monday, June 25, 2018
Defense witnesses presented

Monday, June 25, 2018
Jury handed case for deliberation and decision

Tuesday, June 26, 2018
Jury presents Judge Sams their decision
Guilty all 5 counts

1) Malice Murder (O.C.G.A. 16-5-1) (a)
2) Felony Murder (O.C.G.A. 16-5-1) (c)
3) Aggravated Assault (O.C.G.A. 16-5-21)
4) Aggravated Battery (O.C.G.A. 16-5-24)
5) Concealing Death of Another (O.C.G.A. 16-10-31)

Tuesday, June 26, 2018
Franklin George Gebhardt sentenced to life in prison plus 30-years-probation. Taken from Spalding County Courtroom to jail where he will spend rest of life in prison.

William Franklin Moore Plea Deal

Thursday, August 16, 2018
William Franklin Moore pleads guilty to the murder of Timothy Wayne Coggins.
Sentenced to 20 years in prison plus 10 years supervised probation upon release
1) Voluntary Manslaughter
2) Concealing the Death of Another

Thursday, August 16, 2018
Moore wheeled out of the Spalding County Courtroom
to jail in a wheelchair where he will spend 20 years
in prison.

Thursday, February 14, 2019
Motion for a retrial of Franklin George Gebhardt
heard in Spalding County Superior Court by
Judge W. Fletcher Sams

Thursday, February 21, 2019
Bill Moore meets with author at Johnson State Prison,
Wrightsville, GA for interview

May 2019
Judge Sams denies motion for new trial, Gebhardt

Spring and Summer 2019
Author requests interview with Gebhardt in
Prison in Reidsville. To date (09-17-19) request
has not been granted

Summer, 2019
Georgia Supreme Court asked to consider retrial for
Franklin George Gebhardt

Family Trees
Franklin George Gebhardt

Franklin George Gebhardt
Born 08/19/1959 or 1960

Charles Father…..Evelyn Mother

Girlfriend	Tammy McCully
Child	Franklin Cory Gebhardt (son)
	Born 12/05/1971
Girlfriend	Peggy Ledford
Child	** (daughter)
	Date of Birth and last Name
	Withheld-see ** Notes
Wife	Carole Ann Day Hebeisen
	Born 05/11/1964
	Married 08/11/2006
	Died 07/04/2012

Pauline	Sister
Richard	Brother
Charles	Brother
Sandra	Brother
Franklin George Gebhardt	
Brenda	Sister

William Franklin Moore
Born 05/06/1959

Amos F. Father…Barbara Jean Mother

<u>Sisters</u>
Sandra
Diane
Alisa

<u>Brother</u>
Rodney (d.1981)

Brenda (Gebhardt baby sister)
Married Bill Moore
02/04/1977

-Children with Brenda-
Brandy Moore Abercrombie-1977
Wm. Franklin Moore, Jr.-1981
Divorced Brenda
Married Deborah Ann Watson
January 3, 2003
Divorced Deborah

Wife Brenda Died 2014

End Notes

*Sue Ellen named used in Chapter 4, Deadly Choice at the People's Choice…is not the real name of the white female girlfriend of Timothy Wayne Coggins. Source asked real name not to be used. Author has honored this request.

** ---., used in family tree chart, is the daughter sired by Gebhardt with girlfriend Peggy Ledford. Source asked last name and birthdate not be used. Author has honored this request.

***These sources asked to remain anonymous. The author will honor their requests.

Franklin George Gebhardt and his attorneys were approached a number of times by the author requesting an interview. The author was refused each time and has yet to interview the murderer.

Why not the Death Penalty

Question
Why wasn't the death penalty sought in either or both cases?
Answer
In Georgia the death penalty may be sought by the prosecution and approved by a jury and judge for specific reasons

O.C.G.A. § 17-10-30

 (a)The death penalty may be imposed for the offenses of aircraft hijacking or treason in any case.

(b)In all cases of other offenses for which the death penalty may be authorized, the judge shall consider, or he/she shall include in his instructions to the jury for it to consider, any mitigating circumstances or aggravating circumstances otherwise authorized by law and any of the following statutory aggravating circumstances which may be supported by the evidence:

(1)The offense of murder, rape, armed robbery, or kidnapping was committed by a person with a prior record of conviction for a capital felony;

(2)The offense of murder, rape, armed robbery, or kidnapping was committed while the offender was engaged in the commission of another capital felony or aggravated battery, or the offense of murder was committed while the offender was engaged in the commission of burglary in any degree or arson in the first degree;

(3)The offender, by his act of murder, armed robbery, or kidnapping, knowingly created a great risk of death to more than one person in a public place by means of a weapon or device which would normally be hazardous to the lives of more than one person;

(4)The offender committed the offense of murder for himself or another, for the purpose of receiving money or any other thing of monetary value;

(5)The murder of a judicial officer, former judicial officer, district attorney or solicitor-general, or former district attorney, solicitor, or solicitor-general was committed during or because of the exercise of his or her official duties;

(6)The offender caused or directed another to commit murder or committed murder as an agent or employee of another person;

(7)The offense of murder, rape, armed robbery, or kidnapping was outrageously or wantonly vile, horrible, or inhuman in that it involved torture, depravity of mind, or an aggravated battery to the victim;

(8)The offense of murder was committed against any peace officer, corrections employee, or firefighter while engaged in the performance of his official duties;

(9)The offense of murder was committed by a person in, or who has escaped from, the lawful custody of a peace officer or place of lawful confinement;

(10)The murder was committed for the purpose of avoiding, interfering with, or preventing a lawful arrest or custody in a place of lawful confinement, of himself or another;

(11)The offense of murder, rape, or kidnapping was committed by a person previously convicted of rape, aggravated sodomy, aggravated child molestation, or aggravated sexual battery; or

(12)The murder was committed during an act of domestic terrorism.

While Gebhardt was found guilty of several of the above offenses (Moore plead guilty), there are also reasons in Georgia that the death penalty should not be asked for by a prosecuting attorney.

In what is called "General Considerations", of the O.C.G.A. there are numerous reasons a death penalty verdict should be requested. The main reason the Spalding County District Attorney did not ask for the death penalty in the Gebhardt case was due to the time lapse between the murder and the trial. Thirty-four plus years is a long time.

In Georgia executions are done by lethal injection as opposed to the electric chair, which was used in the past.

Interesting enough, the Georgia Electric Chair was used for many years and was located in the prison in which Gebhardt is now housed, in Reidsville.

Witnesses Subpoenaed for Trial(s)

Witness List State vs **Franklin George Gebhardt**
18-R-105A-Trial Held

No witnesses at plea hearing of **William Franklin Moore**,
Sr. 18-R-105B-Plea Bargain Accepted
Only statement was from Coggins family member
Heather Coggins

Testified for Prosecution
Brandy Abercrombie-Daughter Bill Moore
Johnathan Bennett-In jail w/Gebhardt
Telisa Coggins-Sister Timothy Wayne Coggins
Linda Morgan Cook-Aunt-Tim Coggins
Jared Coleman-GBI Special Agent
Patrick John Douglas-In Jail with Gebhardt
Greg Dubin-Owner Atlanta Hydrovac
Samuel Freeman-Friend of Coggins
Christina Froehlich Kannon-GBI
Jesse Gates-City of Griffin Police Department
Ashley Hinkle-GBI
Oscar Jordan-Investigator SCSO
Mike Morris-Captain SCSO
Larry Peterson-GBI
Clint Phillips-Investigator SCSO
Terry Reed-In jail with Gebhardt
Willard Sanders-Friend of Gebhardt
James Sebestyen-GBI
Robert Eugene Smith-Partied with Gebhardt
Daniella Stuart-GBI
Charles Lloyd Sturgill-Lived at Carey's
Rachael Thornton-GBI
Warren Tillman-GBI
Christopher Joseph Vaughn-Key Witness

Testified for Defense
Samuel Baity-Former GBI
Daniel Greene-Former GBI

Subpoenaed but did not testify

Richard Abercrombie
Ricky Lee Ammons
Gerald Blanton
Charles Bunn
Lamar Bunn-Gebhardt Nephew
Dennis Bunn
Sandra Ruth Bunn-Gebhardt Sister
Larry Dale Campbell-Retired Investigator
Charles Carey, Jr.-Chris Vaughn's father
Bobby Carroll
Tim Clift-Lamar County SO
Tom Davis-GBI
Chris Demarco-GBI
Robert-Devane-GBI
Darrell Dix-Spalding County Sheriff
Keith Duncan-SCSO
Natalie Dianne Duncan
Larry Duren-GBI
Charles Durham
Benny Easterling-Geb. Assault Victim
Luke Ensow
Joshua Foreman-Verizon Wireless
Jane Luke Freer
Maurice Freer
Jennifer Fuller
Evelyn Gaston
Franklin Corey Gebhardt Son-Frankie Gebhardt
Gerald Glanton

Wanda Glanton
Bobby Gene Goolsby
Deanna Gross-GBI
"Mitzie" Guy (Beasley)-Girlfriend of Geb.-Deceased
Barry Lamar Hamm
Phil Hammond-Investigator
Tammy Harmon-Girlfriend of Geb.
Todd Harris-SCSO
Jeff Hatchett-GBI
Todd-Hendrix-Investigator
Raymond Hightower-Investigator
Brenda Hood
Steven Jennings
Dwayne Jones-SCSO
Josh Jones
Laurie Lane
Kenneth Law
K.D. Lowe-GA State Patrol
Keith Massengale-Investigator
Michael P. McCarriagher-GBI
Will Montgomery-GBI
Wm. Franklin Moore, Sr.-Defendant
Casey Moore-Friend of Gebhardt-Deceased
Barbara Bauer Moore-Minix
Pauline Myers Sister-Gebhardt
June S. Nale
Keesha Norman
Jessica Price
Tony Ranieri-SCSO
Beth Reynolds
Timothy Roberts
Diane Sanders
John N. Scoggins
Shirley Sisk
Amy Smallwood

Troy James Smith
Melissa Stamford
Tammy Gail Stansell
Tammy Starckey
David Stevenson
Tony Thomason-SCSO
Willie J. Walker
Zachery Whitmer
Eddie Lewis Williams
Fredrick Wimberly-GBI
Dennis Wynn
Janice Wynn
Camareka Yarbrough-SCSO

My Gypsy Lover
By Quimby Melton III

Here is a sample of another book in the works by the author: Look for it Summer/Fall 2020 amazon.com

+++++++

In the reality of things there are laws of nature and laws of man.

The first, the laws of nature are researched, theorized and defined by scientists. Such things as motion, gravity, orbit of the planets around our sun, ocean waves, sunrise, sunset are all the laws that define our natural universe. Thus, our space is defined with certain, consistent, and explainable clarifications of our being.

For centuries scientists, philosophers and metaphysicians have contemplated what the laws of nature truly are and are not. These are the laws that are explainable yet, have no boundary. New laws of nature are being discovered and analyzed in our modern world at a clip beyond what humankind ever thought possible.

While the laws of nature are explainable, the laws of man, or rather the violation of the rules of man, are unexplainable.

Rules of man guide our society and enhance our natural way of being. Traffic laws, societal well-being, rights and wrong decided by courts based on our laws of man all point toward a harmony of purpose. These are laws of association and cohabitation within our society and should not be broken. If they are consequences come about, just as with laws of nature.

But our society is a strange thing. One person may naturally and with knowledge of obey these laws. Others simply do not. What is right and natural to one is simply abhorrent to another. That is when disharmony, upheaval and dire consequences come about. Simply put, some people may feel they are above the societal needs and laws of man.

Then you have divine law. Preachers for generations have shared the divine law within their pulpits; measured what is sinful and what is righteous; what is moral and amoral; generally, what is accepted by the law of man and what is not.

When the divine speaks, one hopefully listens. Perhaps it is via prophets, perhaps through inspiration within the soul; perhaps by way of a gypsy fortune teller. Who knows what sparks that inner soul to listen? But the spark is there. You pay attention to the divine, even if you forget who you are and why you are here.

The gypsy woman tells you your fortune, you had better listen.

If not, one may be doomed with the curse that can never be taken away.

It is a curse that is lasting. And it is with that curse we begin our story.

+++++++

The old lady with the gnarled hands sat behind a table in the room with the curtains pulled. The room was dark for the middle of the afternoon, but Lady Knight liked it that way. She felt closer to the spirits and voices that had spoken to her most of her adult life.

Her office was in the front of her home. She had gotten the county commission to zone her property commercial several years ago, so she could have both her office and home in the same building. The property was on a main highway, in a part of town that had seen better days. Businesses seemed to move every decade or so, thanks to over eager developers who built new shopping centers and office complexes north of the ever-expanding city. The bargains on property and rentals could be found in this part of town. Shoppers had migrated north to the newer developments. But that was okay with Lady Knight. Her business was thriving none the less.

Her afternoon client was definitely a, "smoothie," someone who did not have callused hands thanks to a high paying office job. In fact, Lady Knight wondered if the man she was meeting to read his palm had ever really done any outside work. His hands were lotion smooth, nails clipped by professionals and a slight scent of the exotic spicy-citrus punch smell of Calvin Klein Man spray. His buttoned-up L.L. Bean shirt had his initials on the pocket, GED. An ironed khaki pair of wool pants fit his slim waist. He enjoyed looking his best, even to have his palm read and future told by the gypsy woman.

Gerald Edward DeLong was on his lunch hour. He seldom carried cash, relying mostly on credit and debit cards. He could earn the airline miles with items charged. But this was not something he wanted to appear on his credit card. His wife, one or the other, might notice the charge. Questions would be asked, an explanation made up, and calamity avoided once again. So, Gerald stopped at the bank and withdrew $150 in cash. It was better this way. No one would know but Lady Knight and him.

The standard rate for a palm reading from Lady Knight was $40, but he knew if she told him, "What he wanted to hear," he would give her a handsome tip.

The duo sat down at a table covered with a tablecloth that had seen better days. But it was dark, DeLong didn't notice, and Lady Knight lacked concern. This was the way she had spoken to the spirits for years and years. She was too old to change now.

"Good afternoon," Lady Knight almost purred in an Eastern European accent. Despite years of living in the North Atlanta suburbs, her friends and family continued to speak to each other in the mother tongue. "It's a pleasure to invite you in. The future my friend is always with us, beside us, and in our souls," she told the middle-aged gentleman as he sat down. She also knew this was perhaps the first time the stranger was having his palm read, for after all these years, Lady Knight could sense a feeling of nervousness from her clients. "Relax my friend and let me see your right hand and palm. Things are not always as we expect them to be. The hands will tell us of your future, maybe good, maybe not. But most of the time good," she shared trying to get DeLong to relax.

As was her habit, Lady Knight took a silk handkerchief from her blouse and wiped the sweat from the palm of the hand. This too was something she had done numerous times with anxious clients.

Always wanting to begin her sessions on a positive note, Lady Knight looked toward the heart line. A long and solid line would indicate an open heart and perhaps life. The heart line on DeLong's palm was solid, curving upward. "You have a strong heart, my friend. You take good care of yourself and your health," she said looking into her client's eyes. DeLong smiled but he knew that he took good care of himself. He exercised hard, several times a week. On his out of town trips he would book upper floor rooms and took the stairs instead of the elevator whenever possible. So, this was not real news to the client. But he would keep an open mind and see if the fortune teller could find why he had really come to her.

Learned from her mother back in the, "old country," Lady Knight would go the right side of the palm and find the money line. This was an old trick to encourage a large tip. If she could predict money, lots of it, in the future, the client might smile and think he was even more successful than they were. But for DeLong, success had come to him long ago. The trick was that he had made it stay with him. "You are very successful," the gypsy woman smiled at the client. "You have money and I see even more in your future. This is a good thing, no?"

"Yes," DeLong replied quickly. "I have been very lucky through the years." But he knew luck had nothing to do with it. He was resourceful, quick and able to be as cutthroat as any pirate who sailed the Caribbean seas. Time after time he would sell to the unsellable. Close the deal that no one else could close. It took a sixth sense, but DeLong had the balls and guts to get things done. His status rose in the company time and again. He was without peer when it came to his job…and he knew it.

Next came the marriage line. This is where Lady Knight got out her spectacles. "I see something very interesting here," she told her client. "Are you married, or have you ever been married before?" Most of the times Lady Knight would look for a wedding ring as a client entered her room. But today there was none to be found. Only a college ring, heavy, gold, with a UGA seal was seen on the right hand. "Yes, I'm married," DeLong quickly replied, with an almost nervous high-pitched voice. "How can you tell?"

"This line here," Lady Knight pointed out. "It is deep and strong and then gets weak, then strong again."

"No. Happily married," DeLong replied trying to convince himself.

But what Lady Knight saw she did not ask. There were definite secrets within the marriage line. Where there should have been one line, there were two distinct crossing lines. In her years of advisement, she had only seen this one other time, and it was when she first began her, "prophecy," That had not turned out very well for her, or her client.

"No…no. I see now," Lady Knight feigned with another response looking even more closely at the marriage line. "It is a good line, a good marriage. You are a happy man. I can see that." But Lady Knight knew what she had seen. A highly unusual double line. "I will move on if okay with you," the oracle suggested. DeLong agreed. Better to leave that line alone.

Lady Knight then moved toward the head-line. As she looked closely at the line she said, "You have a strong will. You know what you want in life. You are not easily changed with your mind,"

DeLong smiled inwardly, trying not to admit the clairvoyant had him pegged. He did know what he wanted. But what he wanted to know was the why. Why was he the way he was? He knew what he was doing was against not only the laws of man, the laws of the church, but also against the laws of common sense. But he also knew that this too was a challenge to him. That he could not stop without monumental circumstances being upended. Lives would be changed, forever. These were things, once started could never be stopped. Like Pandora's Box, once released, it could never be contained again. He simply could not stop…at least for now.

"You smile. You agree," Lady Knight said as she looked into DeLong's eyes.

"Yes, I agree. I know what I want," DeLong smiled back.

"Then let's take a last look at your palm. Your fate. What is your fate on this special day?" the visionary spoke. Lady Knight also had learned from her mother that this was a good way to end a session. Even if fate did not favor the client, she would gloss over or create a happier scenario for her paying customer. Another session, a better tip. Everyone wants to know they fate. It was as natural as having your palm read.

"Let me look," Lady Knight spoke in an almost low guttural voice. The fate line is almost dead center in the palm. DeLong's line began strong but what took Lady Knight's breath away was how suddenly it stopped. DeLong could not help but hear the gasp. "Anything wrong," he asked. "Errrr, no nothing sir. It's just I haven't seen a fate line like this in a long time." The gypsy woman looked up and gave a smile. "No sir. Nothing wrong. In fact, it is one of the strongest fate lines I have seen," she lied. But as with numerous clients, the old lady could have been an actress. "You see how strong your line begins. This is good. Better than good, sir. You will determine your own destiny. Fate smiles on you today." But in her heart the gypsy knew better. A line that suddenly stops is a sure sign of tragedy. A sign of permanence. Perhaps even a sign of death. No, the play must go on. There would only be good news for her client today.

"Sir, destiny rests with you and you alone. You are master of your domain and all that lies within."

Satisfied, Gerald Edward DeLong rose from his chair. The gypsy woman had confirmed all that he wanted verified. He was in control of his own destiny. He was the master and commander of his life. A full, but mixed up life, by standards of the norms. The gypsy woman had told him that he was in control of his own fate, his own destiny, his own life. Yes, he knew that he was a restless spirit and that for most people his relationships would not have worked. But he was Gerald Edward DeLong and the confirmation today, from the seer was what mattered. He could continue his life as he wished, as mixed up and crazy as it might be for others, it was okay for him.

"Sir. I hope I have not disappointed today," Lady Knight spoke, with the appearance of humbleness. Surely her mother would have been proud.

"Disappointed? Not at all. In fact, I am extremely relieved with what you told me today," DeLong said in an almost joyous tone. "Couldn't be better. Couldn't be better," he smiled.

DeLong reached in his pocket and handed Lady Knight four twenty-dollar bills. Quickly folding the money and gently placing it into her bosom, the gypsy woman knew she had been tipped well. "Thank you, sir. It has been my pleasure. And I hope our souls will meet again."

As DeLong left the room and entered the front part of the office, he turned around, facing the old woman. Her poker face did not give her away. "Perhaps another session soon. As our destiny and fate allows," DeLong smiled.

With that he took his blue blazer coat and went out the front door to his BMW. From here he would head back to the office. He had another sales trip in two days. He would never reveal his secret and he knew the gypsy woman would not either. His tip had seen to that.

But as the door shut, Lady Knight knew what was real and what was coming. She knew an unpleasant fate awaited her client. He seemed like a nice young man, but there was something. Something about a life that seemed oh so perfect. Scared for both the future and her client, Lady Knight said a silent prayer to the Virgin:

Gula Devla, da me saschipo. Swuntuna Devla, da me bacht t'aldaschis cari me jav; te ferin man, Devla, sila ta niapaschiata, chungale manuschendar, ke me jav ande drom ca hin man traba; ferin man, Devia; ma mek man Devla, ke manga man tre Devies-key.

Sweet Goddess, give him health. Holy Goddess, give him luck and grace wherever he may go; and help him, Goddess, powerful and immaculate, from ugly men, that I may go in the road to the place I purpose: help him, Goddess; forsake him not, Goddess, for I pray for God's sake. From: The Zincali by George Barrow

His secret was so deep that he dared not even pray about it…not that DeLong was a religious man to start with.

OQMIII

Photographs

The Victim and the Murderers
Timothy Wayne Coggins (top left photo) was savagely murdered by Franklin George Gebhardt (bottom left) and William Franklin Moore (top right). A Spalding County jury found Gebhardt guilty on all five counts he was charged with on June 26, 2018. Bill Moore pled guilty two months later and received 20 years in prison with another 10-years' probation. *Photos courtesy of the family and taken by the author*

Moore seemed repentant

A repentant William Franklin Moore being wheeled away immediately after pleading guilty to the murder of Timothy Wayne Coggins. Moore would be sentenced to 20 years in prison with another 10 years' probation. Judge Sams wanted Moore to serve even more time but went along with the wishes of the family and district attorney. Photo taken August 2018. *Photo by the author*

Fire and rage from the beginning of the case

Frankie Gebhardt enters the magistrate courtroom for the first day of hearings on November 30, 2017. At no time did the convicted murderer seem remorseful or repentant that he had killed Timothy Wayne Coggins. *Photo by the author*

Slain man identified

A man found slain Sunday has been identified as Timothy Wayne Coggins, 23, of 635 E. Solomon St., Griffin, Sheriff James Freeman said today. He said identification was made through crime lab fingerprints and other data gathered during an investigation.

The body of Coggins was found off Minter Road in the northern part of Spalding County near the Beaverbrook Airport. Stab wounds and other evidence suggested violent death, Freeman said.

He said the investigation continued today.

"We'll follow the trail to wherever it leads," the sheriff said. State crime lab people have been assisting with the investigatiion.

Personal data about the slain man was being gathered today, the Spalding Sheriff said.

He said the next of kin were being notified.

News story about the identification of the murder victim, Timothy Wayne Coggins, *Griffin Daily News*, Tuesday, October 11, 1983. *Courtesy Griffin Daily News files*

Deaths, funerals

Mr. Coggins

Funeral services for Mr. Timothy Wayne Coggins will be Friday at 2 p.m. in the Fuller Chapel United Methodist Church in Zebulon. The Rev. Jeremiah Lyons will officiate. Burial will be in the church cemetery.

Survivors include his mother, Mrs. Viola Dorsey; father, Marshall Lawrence; stepfather, Robert Lee Dorsey; four sisters, Mrs. Peggy Richard, Miss Harriette Coggins, Miss Telisa Coggins and Miss Jacqueline Coggins, all of Griffin; three brothers, Eugene Coggins, Dwayne Coggins, both of Griffin and Ramon Coggins of Atlanta; grandparents, Mr. and Mrs. Robert Lawrence of Milner; eight aunts, eight uncles, nieces and nephews.

Friends may visit the family at 635 E. Solomon St. McDowell United Funeral Home is in charge of plans.

Mrs. Frye

Mrs. Charlotte Fogg Frye of 518 E. College St., died Wednesday morning at the Griffin-Spalding Hospital. She was the widow of Dr. Augustus H. Frye Sr.

Mrs. Frye was born in Kansas City, Kan., and was a member of the First Baptist Church. She was past president of the Wisteria Garden Club, past president of the Griffin Camera Club and was a member of the 99 Flying Club, along with Amelia Earhart.

She is survived by two sons, Samuel Warren Frye of Griffin and Dr. Augusta H. Frye Jr., of Chattanooga, Tenn.; daughter, Mrs. Barbara Hothorn of High Point, N. C.; six grandchildren and four great-grandchildren; and a sister, Mrs. Julia Weems of Jacksonville, Fla.

Funeral services will be Saturday at 2 p.m. in Haisten's Funeral Home chapel. Burial will be in Oak Hill Cemetery. Haisten's Funeral Home is in charge.

Mrs. Huckaby

Mrs. Opal Faye Huckaby, 74, of 368 Wisso Road died Wednesday evening at the Living Center of Griffin.

Mrs. Huckaby was a member of the Teamon Baptist Church and was a Sunday School teacher for 20 years.

Timothy Wayne Coggins Obituary in the Thursday, October 13, 1983 issue of the Griffin Daily News.
Courtesy Griffin Daily News files

Fuller Chapel United Methodist Church, Zebulon, GA
Photo by the author

IN LOVING MEMORY
TIMOTHY WAYNE
COGGINS
AUGUST 29, 1960
OCTOBER 9, 1983
"GONE, BUT NEVER FORGOTTEN"

Timothy Wayne Coggins' marked grave, behind Fuller Chapel United Methodist Church, early 2018. The grave site had been unmarked for 34 plus years because family and friends were afraid it would be desecrated and destroyed by the ruthless murderers and their friends.

Photo by the author

Crime Lab Investigator Larry Peterson (l) documented potential clues near the site where an unidentified black male was found dead of multiple stab wounds. The body was located in a field off Minter Road near Mobley, about 400 feet directly behind Peterson. Sheriff Freeman (center) points out other possible evidence sites to Inv. Clint Phillips.

Photograph of the crime scene which appeared in the *Griffin Daily News* Monday, October 10, 1983. Investigators would find the body of a then unknown young black man covered in blood the day before. It appeared the body had been drug through the farmland and stabbed numerous times. Investigators noted, whoever the victim was, had died a, "violent death," at the hands of someone who wanted him (the victim) "savagely," killed. Reporter Carl Elmore covered the story for the *Griffin Daily News*.

Courtesy Griffin Daily News files

To the Bench for Discussion

Judge W. Fletcher Sams ran an orderly courtroom during the Gebhardt and Moore trials. Seen at Judge Sams' bench is, (l-r) Marie Broder, Spalding County Assistant District Attorney, Larkin Lee and Scott Johnston, Frankie Gebhardt's defense attorneys.

Photo by the author

Prosecution Team

Spalding County was well represented with Assistant District Attorney Marie Broder (left) and Spalding County District Attorney Ben Coker. Even after 34 long, tortuous years of anguish and agony for the family and community the prosecution never relented in finding the true facts of the murder bringing both Gebhardt and Moore to justice.

Photo by the author

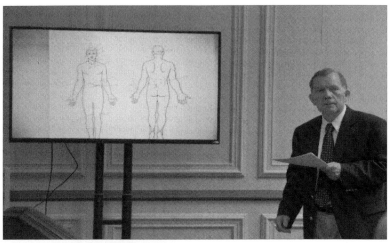

Courtroom Testimony

In the top photo Warren Tillman, original medical examiner for the state, shows a diagram where Timothy Wayne Coggins was stabbed...as many as 38 times. Stab wounds are both in the front and back of the body. Notice the "X" mark on the body. In the lower photograph, Telisa Coggins cries as she testifies about the night, she tried to rescue her brother from the People's Choice nightclub.

Photo by the author

Arrested, booked and charged
In the photographs above (top left) Gregory Huffman, Sandra Bunn (top right) and Lamar Bunn (bottom right) were arrested and charged with, "Obstruction of Justice." All three made bail. Both Huffman and Lamar Bunn lost their law enforcement jobs due to their arrests. Sandra Bunn continued to maintain that her baby brother, Frankie, was "innocent," even after the jury returned their verdict of murder and Gebhardt was incarcerated in Reidsville.

Photos courtesy Spalding County Sheriff's Office

No Strangers to jail
Neither Bill Moore (left 1994) nor Gebhardt (bottom-1983) were strangers to the Georgia Penal System. They had 70 plus arrests between them.

Photos courtesy Georgia Department of Corrections

Sheriff Darrell Dix (left) Captain Mike Morris (middle) and GBI Special Agent Jared Coleman worked day and night to solve the murder. *Photos by the author*

Court comes to order Judge Rita Cavanaugh (left) ruled at the preliminary hearing there was enough evidence to bind the Coggins murder case over to the Spalding County Grand Jury. In the top photo, Bailiffs William Matchett (l-r) Barbara Puerifoy and Jim Goolsby kept order in the Superior Court. *Photos by the author*

Nightclub
These are photos of the People's Choice club where a trio of white thugs picked Coggins up and later killed him. *Photos by the author*

Investigators scoured scene Several investigators were crucial to the Coggins murder case in 1983. Jesse Gates (top left) worked with the City of Griffin Police Department. He would give his friend Timothy Wayne Coggins a ride to the People's Choice. Clint Phillips (middle) went to the scene of the crime October 9, 1983. Oscar Jordan (bottom left), was hired as a liaison between the black community and the Spalding County Sheriff's Department. *Photos by the author*

Evidence found in bottom of dry well
Evidence was presented during Frankie Gebhardt's trial that showed several items thrown down the bottom of a dried water well near his home. Daniella Stuart and Marie Broder show the jurors a shoe (top left photo) and a chain (bottom left) that were found in the bottom of the well. Coggins wore a size 10 Adidas shoe (top left). Christina Froehlich Kannon, GBI agent, (bottom right) shows one of the knives found at the bottom of the well. Gebhardt (top right) shows his concern as the items are revealed to the jury.

Photos by the author

Photos by the author

Rogue's Gallery

It was a rogue's gallery at the Gebhardt Trial. Christopher Joseph Vaughn (top left) witnessed Gebhardt and Coggins arguing at Carey's Trailer Park when he was 10 years old. Johnathan Bennett (top middle), Robert Eugene Parker (top right) and Patrick Douglas (bottom left) witnessed Gebhardt bragging about the murder while in jail. Longtime friend, Willard Sanders, (bottom right) overheard Gebhardt brag about the murder at a party.

Together again

Gebhardt and Moore appeared together again at the March 2018 hearing. Gebhardt crying during his trial when his late wife's name was mentioned.

Photos by the author

Photos by the author

"Thank you sweet Jesus"
The long wait was over. The Coggins family and law enforcement hug in top photo. Heather Coggins (left) was spokeslady for the family. Bottom photo Telisa Coggins hugs Marie Broder at end of the trial. "Thank you sweet Jesus," Telisa cried.

Franklin George Gebhardt will spend the rest of his life in prison. William Franklin Moore will spend 20 years in prison. *Photo by the author*

Made in the
USA
Columbia, SC